Manna Stories:
Journeys Toward the Heart of Jesus Christ

B.Z. Eliphaz

Copyright © 2014 Jon Schlueter
All rights reserved.

ISBN: 0692346716
ISBN-13: 9780692346716

Published by:
142 Company
22421 Barton Road, #354
Grand Terrace, California 92313

142 Company is a d/b/a of Jon Schlueter

(E-mail) **MannaStories@Yahoo.com**

(Website) **BZEliphaz.com**

To Mom and Dad,
who loved me.

CONTENTS

Introduction		7
1.	BELIEF	9
2	VESTMENT	28
3	TRADE	37
4	ALL	46
5	MULTITUDES	53
6.	PLUCK	72
7.	GIANT	85
8.	THIRST	98
9.	PITY	109
10.	TURMOIL	118
11.	FORTUNE	137
12.	CALLING	151
Afterword		159

Introduction

In Gospel times, Jesus met people and changed lives. The New Testament Gospels tell many stories like that. Some of these stories are jewel-like: tiny and brilliant. They're told in only a few sentences. We meet the people in these stories only briefly.

This book elaborates these jewel-like stories. The pieces in this book imagine the lives of the people we meet in these stories before they met Jesus. And they imagine what happened to them afterward. They imagine the meeting itself in more detail.

Sometimes, these Gospel stories become blurred by familiarity. I hope that these elaborations will caffeinate any tired familiarity. I hope that these elaborations will inspire a reader to go back to the Bible with refreshed wonder. The idea of these elaborations is that the Bible is an amazing book that rewards deep reading.

Conversation about these Gospel stories has gone on, sometimes serenely, sometimes ferociously, for two-thousand years. These elaborations might toss some ideas into that conversation. Maybe they'll inspire you to add to that conversation, or to add something different than you have in the past.

So far as I know, only the eighth story, "Thirst," borrows from a tradition. In that case, it is a tradition of the Orthodox Church.

I've tried to amplify these stories faithfully to my understanding of the Lord, the Lion and the Lamb, the ruler of the rulers of the earth. I invite you to read these stories and draw your own conclusions about their faithfulness to the Gospels.

And, please, read the Gospel stories that are the bedrock of this book. Decide how you would elaborate those stories, especially if your ideas differ from mine.

I hope that I have been respectful to the people described in these elaborations. That's because, for one thing, I hope to meet them one day.

Men and women followed Jesus around two-thousand years ago and saw with their own eyes wonderful stories. What was true then is true today. I try in this book to capture a little of that wonder.

The word of God is wild. Perhaps these elaborations reflect that wildness. They cannot contain it.

B.Z. Eliphaz

1

BELIEF

Matt. 17:1-21; Mark 9:2-29; Luke 9:28-43

"My father did not know that Jesus's clothes had become brilliant white, nor that his face had changed and shone with the spirit of God. He did not know that Moses and Elijah had talked with Jesus on the small mountain that rose out of the plain where we stood among his disciples.

"We would learn that later."

The man speaking was in his early-thirties. He had unkempt brown hair and the untidy beard of a traveler. He was neither tall nor short, not hefty and not small.

The three-dozen men around him were armed like fortresses. Some of them glanced from time to time at the left side of his face. Some stared openly.

"Before anything else, I remember my father stooping among his vines and cutting bunches of fat, dark-purple grapes. He would do this from sun-up to sun-down. He paused only to wipe the sweat from his face with the back of his big hand, or to gaze at his young wife and his little boy. Sometimes he lifted his eyes to heaven to praise God, who had given him all things needed for life and happiness.

"He and my mother would teach me the words of scripture, which they too had learned as children. They taught me Joshua's words:

> But if you don't wish to serve the Lord, then today choose whom you will serve – the gods that your ancestors served beyond the river, or the gods of the Amorites in whose land you stand. As for me and my house, we will serve the Lord.

"Things changed. In my seventh winter, father and I were in our small stone house. He was talking to me about planting and reaping. I suddenly became unaware of him – of him or of anything else. This lasted for only a short time. Afterward, I did not know that anything had happened. These events started to come often. My parents began to watch for them.

"Then, in the harvest season of the same year, father and I were walking among the hanging grapes. He was showing me how to know when to take the bunches from the vines. He pointed out the color. He taught me to crush a grape between my finger and thumb to tell its firmness. He had me chew a grape to measure its thick juiciness. He told me what to expect when I tasted the flavor in its skin.

"We walked between rows of grapes. He became aware that I had not kept up with him. He found me on the ground between two rows of vines. I shook, my mouth foamed, and I was grinding my teeth. He was afraid.

"When I stopped shaking and foaming, he carried me in his arms to our small house. I put my arms around his neck. I cried because my head hurt so much.

"After that, this unclean spirit afflicted me so often that I didn't cry, even when I would fall and strike my head.

"My father took me to physicians, but they did not help.

"I grew worse. In my ninth year, I was alone in our house and it happened again. When I came to myself, I tried to stand, but my legs wobbled. I lurched for the table to keep from falling. As I did that, my hand hit the table and upset a clay pot. It fell to the floor. I saw it break into pieces, but I heard nothing.

"My little mother rushed into the house when she heard the pot break. In terror, I pointed to my ears and told her I could not hear. I could not even hear myself tell her that. I saw her press her fists to her cheeks. She opened her mouth wide, as if she were wailing.

"Six months later, my father gestured to me to come with him to the fields while he trimmed the vines to give the growing grapes more sun. I followed him. But as we walked I suddenly lost track of where we were going. I tried to call to my father, but I could not form words. When I could not cry out to my father, I tried to cry out to God. I could not do that, either.

"I sat where I was in silent fright. After a time, my father came back to look for me. I looked up into his tired eyes, and I pointed to my mouth. I shook my head. He understood. He kneeled and hugged my head to his chest.

"Every year, my father took a lamb or a goat to the local priest to offer to God. He could not afford that; we went without so that he could make these sin offerings. The priest would tie the legs of the lamb or goat. He would hold shut its mouth as he cut deeply into its throat. Afterward, I was still deaf and mute, and the spirit still tormented me.

"I was twelve when a stranger came. It was winter. Father was sitting cross-legged under an oak tree. The stranger was about 40 years old, eight years older than my father. He was dressed in a costly linen tunic and a brown wool cloak embroidered with green designs above its fringe. My father stood as the stranger approached.

"The stranger drew up to my father. He said, 'I have heard of your son's suffering. I am a father. You are a father. I ask you: Would you accept my help for the sake of your son's well-being, even though I am a stranger to you?'

"My father looked at him with curiosity and hope. He said, 'Yes, I would.' They sat down together.

"The stranger asked to see me. My father brought me out to him. When he saw me, the stranger snaked his tongue between his upper and lower lips.

"My mother brought bread and a stew made with lentils and set them before this man. After he had put down the empty bowl, the stranger said 'I am from a village to the north. I have always been troubled when I see suffering like your son's. I am troubled that there is no help for it.'

"My father studied the man's face.

"The man continued: 'I worship the Lord like you do. But I have made a careful study of suffering, like your son's suffering, and like your own. After years and much prayer, I have learned things.

"'Painfully, this is what I have learned: Our God has no power over demons like the one that harms your son. This is also plain: the God we worship has a deep love for people like you and your family. Ours is a good God. In truth, his love runs deeper than his jealousy.

"'As I said, I am from the north. I know the men from beyond Galilee, men from Tyre and Sidon. I know their cleverness. I know their skill at building, at sailing, at trading. I know the wealth of their cities.' With a shrug, he gestured at our rustic stone house. Then he gestured at me.

"'I know a man. He has power to call on the god from the north, the Baal of Tyre and Sidon. This Baal is a clever god, like the men of Tyre and Sidon are clever.

"'I promise you this: If you and your house would only worship Baal, then this priest would call upon Baal for you.

He would make your son well. And also, if you worship this clever god of these clever people, then you will prosper and grow rich, like the men of Tyre and Sidon.'

"Father stood up. The stranger stood, too. The stranger quickly said, 'Of course, you can still worship God. But for your son's sake, remember the great love of God, which makes him welcome help from other gods to heal his beloved people.'

"My father raised his voice and told the stranger to go. Spittle flecked his beard.

"As he left, the stranger shouted over his shoulder 'Think of what I have said! Think! After you have thought, you will see me again!'

"My suffering continued. One day, the unclean spirit seized me next to the pond on my father's vineyard. I fell into the pond. It was good fortune that sometimes I would scream without being aware of it when the demon entered me. That happened next to the pond; my father heard and came running. He pulled me out of the water.

"Later, I fell into the water again. After that, I had to stay away from the water.

"As he had promised, the stranger came back. After the vines had bled, he came back with another man. They came while my father was alone in the vineyard inspecting new buds.

"This time, the first stranger stayed silent. The other man spoke. He was older, grey, and gaunt. He asked after my welfare. My father said little, but he did not tell them to go away.

"The man said, 'Listen. My friend was wrong. Consider your son. Consider history. Consider how hard you work to wrest your livelihood from the ground. The God you worship is a powerful God, but he is not a loving God.

"'Think on the famous wealth of the cities to the north. Baal and Astarte are the gods of these cities, of Tyre and Sidon. These gods are kind. They are generous. They would save your son even if your own indifferent God will not.'

"My father did not yell at them. He asked them to leave. The new stranger said, 'Remember King Solomon. He built alters to Astarte. It is she that I speak of. You are a grape-grower. Are you wiser than King Solomon?'

"They left, but they promised to come back.

"One night shortly after that, my father and a neighbor made a fire between their vineyards to burn vine debris. As I watched flames leap into the air from the dead vegetation, I was seized by the unclean spirit. I plunged into the fire. My father pulled me out. He burned his hands, feet, and forearms. I have the scars that you see.

"The strangers returned one evening shortly before the Feast of the Tabernacles. They brought a third stranger. His red robe and black cloak were unadorned. He was older than the other two. His white hair and beard were storm-like. His eyes penetrated.

"My father sat under the oak, with his back against it. The three strangers stood on three sides of him.

"The third stranger stood directly in front of Father. As he spoke, the others bowed their heads. He said, 'I am a priest and an oracle. These men can tell you that the future is revealed to me. And I can tell you something about your son.'

"My father stood.

"The Oracle continued. 'If nothing changes, you son will not live to the end of the grape harvest.'

"My father's eyes widened. He walked away from the men for about a dozen steps, paused, then turned around and came back. He said, 'Give me seven days to think.'

"The Oracle said, 'It might already be too late.'

"My father said, 'Seven days. Please.'

"Father spoke with my mother. He laid before her what the Oracle had said.

"She was silent for a time. Then she said, 'I am tired like you are tired, and I am afraid like you are.

"'You should go to a teacher, to a scribe. Not the one in our village. He has no answers that have helped. Go to a larger town – Nain perhaps. If the teacher there has a solution, fine. Otherwise, it might be time to make peace with our son's affliction.' They looked at each other's faces for half-a-minute. Then my father nodded his head.

"My father and I left for Nain. It was over half-a-day of steady walking before we saw Nain and the low hill behind it. Men in the synagogue told my father how to find the town's scribe. He was a blacksmith.

"My father found the scribe's house in part by following the directions that the men in the synagogue had given him. But after a time, the clang of metal-on-metal told him where to go.

"From a distance, we saw that the scribe was at his forge under a sheltering roof held up by four posts. He was raising his hammer and smashing it down. Every so often, he would thrust the piece that he was hammering into his furnace and pump his bellows. When we got closer, we saw that he was hammering a piece of metal shaped like a great bird's beak. It was a plow-blade. As we walked up, he inspected the blade and plunged it into a basin of water.

"The scribe was a large man, like my father. They were about the same age. He put his work aside and invited my father to sit with him on the grass in the shade of his house. We sat with him a dozen feet from his bellows and furnace.

"My father described my affliction and its history. He asked the scribe what he should do. The scribe did not answer right away. He rubbed the backs of his thick fingers against the sides of his dark beard. Then he asked my father about himself and about me. He listened keenly to my father's answers, and then he asked more questions based on what my father said. This went on for over two hours.

"Finally, the scribe asked my father if there was anything else. He invited my father to think carefully. He and my father sat silently for several minutes. Then my father answered, 'No.'

"They sat in silence for another quarter-hour. Then my father asked, 'Why is this happening to my boy?'

"The scribe sat without speaking while you might count to ten. Then he said, 'Listen.' He recited a psalm. The psalm starts with questions:

> My God, why do you fling us away for all time?
> Why does your fury immolate the flock of your hand?

"He said, 'The psalm tells of how our enemies brought hatchets and hammers and fire into our temple in Jerusalem. They took the stones that made our meeting-place with God, and they made those stones only stones again. Then they destroyed every other meeting-place of God in the land.'

"'The psalm grieves the absence of signs, prophets, and any person who might have given us hope. Our land was deaf and mute.' He glanced at me.

"My father lowered his head.

"Then the scribe said, 'But listen to the psalm that follows after that one.' He recited the psalm that starts:

> We thank you, O Lord, we thank you,
> Your name is near; people praise your wondrous works.

"My father sat still. Then, the scribe recited another psalm, the one that starts, 'The Lord is my shepherd, I shall not want.' Then he asked, 'Do you know the psalm before that one?'

"My father thought; then he answered, 'I don't remember.'

"The scribe recited the psalm that starts, 'My God, my God, why have you abandoned me?'

"From his expression, it was hard to tell what my father was thinking. Then he said, 'I have a psalm, too.'

"The scribe urged him: 'Please.'

"My father recited this:

> You, O God, have proved us –
> You have refined us like silver.
> You brought us into prison.
> You put shackles on us.
> You made men ride over us.
> We went through fire and water,
> But you brought us into an open space.

"The scribe nodded. He glanced at his bellows. Then he said, 'Do this. Go to the widow who lives outside of this town. Look for a house with an olive tree in front and fields for wheat behind, on the road to Mount Tabor. Speak with her.'

"The scribe said a blessing over us, and we left. We followed his directions. Outside of town, we saw the house with the olive tree. A young man saw us coming. He went inside the house and brought out a woman.

"When we came to them, my father said, 'The teacher sent us.'

"The woman asked, 'Jesus sent you?'

"My father was startled. He said, 'I don't know the teacher Jesus. The teacher from town sent us. The blacksmith.'

"The widow invited us to sit next to the olive tree in the fading light. She brought out water and bread. My father described the brutality of the spirit that harmed me. The widow studied his face as he spoke.

"Then the widow said that Jesus had helped her, and he could help us.

"My father asked, 'Who is Jesus?'

"'Jesus is the man who brought my son back to life.' She gestured toward the glad-seeming, curly-haired man who sat with us. He was about seventeen-years old, and he watched my father and me with large, keen eyes under bushy brows.

"My father asked, 'What do you mean, brought your son "back to life"?'

"Her calm smile and glad eyes were those of a woman who was about to share a wonderful secret with a friend. 'My son was dead. Now he's alive. Jesus did that.'

"My father stared blankly at her.

"She leaned into my father's face, so that her nose was a hand's width away from his. Her eyes were wide open. She lowered her voice. 'I was on the way to bury my son. He was on a funeral bier. He was prepared for burial. His hands and feet were tied with linen strips, and his face was covered with a cloth.

"'Men were carrying him down to his grave next to the road that leads up to Nain. Women were keening behind us. I was in front. Jesus was coming up the road to the town. He and his followers met us just as we came through the town gate.'

"She continued, 'Jesus and his followers stopped and stepped aside. As I approached Jesus, he said for me not to weep. Then he walked past me to the bier and touched it. The men carrying my son stood still.'

"Father asked, 'He touched the bier?' He was surprised.

"The widow answered 'Yes. And then he told my son to rise. Which he did. My son sat up. The men put the bier down and jumped away. They almost dropped my son.'

"The young man grinned and nodded. He looked at my Father, hovered his hand a couple of feet above the ground, and he slapped his palm down to the hard dirt.

"His mother continued with the story. 'And Jesus took the cloth off of my son's face and unbound my son's hands. As he did that, the men who had carried the bier untied the strips of cloth that bound my son's feet.

"'Then Jesus took my son's hand, and my son stood up. Jesus led him to me. He put my son's hand in my hand. I was trembling. I couldn't speak. But my son was jubilant. He shouted praises into the air even as he hugged me.'

"Father looked at the woman, then at her son, then at me, then back at her. He asked, 'Could this be true?'

"She said, 'Listen. My son and I are getting ready to go to Mount Tabor. We leave in the morning. Jesus is there now. Come with us, and you can see for yourself.'

"My father lowered his head and clasped the top of his head with his hands. He was silent for a time.

"We left for Mount Tabor when the sun rose. The weather grew warm because there were no clouds to cast shadows. On the way, father asked the woman to tell the story of Jesus and her son again. He asked many questions.

"In mid-afternoon, we came to a crowd on the northwest side of Mount Tabor. As we approached the crowd, the woman said, 'I don't see the Teacher, but I see his disciples.' She greeted the disciples, and they were glad to see her.

"My father studied the disciples. They dressed simply. Some of them were even a little tattered.

"They were not exalted men. They were sweaty-vineyard men, haggling-marketplace men. They were sunburnt hands that pulled heavy nets into fishing boats.

"In her presence, the disciples told the crowd about the widow of Nain and her son. Soon, she was answering questions from those who had come to see Jesus.

"After she had answered questions for much of an hour, she brought Father and me to the disciples. Father told them why he had come. He asked if he could see Jesus. A disciples said that Jesus had climbed Mount Tabor to pray, and that he had left that morning at sunrise.

"But he said, 'You don't have to wait for him. We have authority to cast out demons. We've had this authority from the Almighty ever since Jesus sent us out in pairs to towns and villages to heal the sick and to cast out demons. When we came back, Jesus had said that he had seen Satan fall from heaven.'

"I was in front of father, and he had his hands on my shoulders. He asked the disciple who said this, 'Please, would you help my boy? He has suffered for so long that it is hard to imagine him without his torment. But listening to this woman' – he looked to the widow of Nain, who stood next to him – 'She has made me hope. So have you.'

"The disciple fixed his eye on me. The crowd grew still. The disciple said, 'Deaf-and-mute spirit, come out of this boy!'

Someone in the crowd asked, 'Did something happen?'

"The disciple spoke to me, but I couldn't hear him. He appeared puzzled. I twisted around and looked at my father. He looked at me. He looked disappointed.

"A second disciple stepped forward. The first disciple stepped back. The second disciple asked, 'Unclean spirit, what is your name?' I saw his lips move, but, just like with the first disciple, that only confused me. He seemed to be talking to me, and I wondered why.

"The first disciple told the second disciple, 'He's deaf. He can't hear you.' Another disciple on his other side said, 'He's mute. He couldn't speak to you, either.' The disciple standing in front of me looked at each of them and nodded his head. I looked behind me, up at my father. He looked sad and tired.

"The disciples conferred together. They told my father that they would try again later.

"We spent the night next to Mount Tabor. Some in the crowd had tents. But Father and I slept in the open.

"The next morning, sick people from the crowd presented themselves to the disciples. The disciples anointed them with oil, and they were healed. Father saw this, and it made him hopeful again. But the disciples tried again to cast the demon out of me, and they failed.

"The next day was sunny, as it had been the day before, and the day before that. But in mid-morning, a dark cloud quickly came down from the top of Mount Tabor and covered the mountain. Everyone backed away. Even though we were next to it, we couldn't see Mount Tabor for the cloud.

"I couldn't hear, but father told me later that there was thunder. There was lightning, too. The cloud was a dense grey, but the lightning made it, for the blink of an eye, brilliantly white. I could feel the earth shake under my feet. Some people said that they heard long blasts from a trumpet. Others heard only the thunder.

"People covered their ears. Some fell face-down on the ground. Some hid in their tents, and others raced away from the mountain.

"The thunder and lightning stopped. The cloud disappeared. Light and warmth dazzled us.

"People came out of their tents. The ones who had flung themselves down stood up, and the ones who had run away came back. Everybody gazed at the rainbow over the mountain.

"For a time, people talked about what had just happened. But when the immediate excitement of the cloud and the lightning and the thunder had waned, all of the disciples who were there at the foot of the mountain surrounded me. Together they worked to free me from my torment. Still, they could not cast out the demon.

"Then three men from the crowd came and stood between the disciples and me. The first man complained to the disciples that they were wrong to do what they were trying to do.

"He said, 'The boy's parents must have sinned, or he himself sinned. That's why a deaf-and-mute spirit harms him. Ask his father about his impiety, or about his lack of faith, because it made his son deaf to God. You men are trying to interfere with heaven's judgment.' My father winced.

"Then the second scribe said, 'His father should say whether the boy was a liar or a blasphemer. The Almighty, in his vast power and deep wisdom, has rebuked him by taking away his power of speech!' Some of the crowd murmured that this was right.

"My father began to protest, but the three scribes shouted him down. The third scribe said, 'There is one cure, and only one cure. A goat or a lamb must be sacrificed. It is a sin offering, as written in the book of Leviticus. Anything else will fail.'

"The disciples argued back. But the scribes said, 'If you can cast out this demon, then cast it out!' The argument spread into the crowd, and soon almost everyone was engaged in a fury of shouting.

"Father did not join in the argument. He sat on the ground and wept into his hands. He sobbed, over and over, that he only wanted his son to be well. The widow of Nain knelt next to him. He did not see her, and he could not hear her above the shouting.

"Years of sorrow had bent his thoughts toward hopelessness. Any path toward hope always circled back to where it had started, as it did at that moment.

"In the chaos of shouting, Jesus and three other disciples came upon us from the direction of Mount Tabor. When the crowd became aware of him, they stopped shouting at each other, and the scribes and the disciples stopped arguing. The crowd ran to Jesus and begged to know what had happened on the mountain.

"Jesus didn't say. He wanted to know what the shouting was about.

"Other people had been crowding forward to speak with Jesus. But when they saw that he was vexed, and when they heard what he asked, they drew back.

"My father walked up to Jesus. He said that he had brought his son to him because I had a demon. He said that the disciples had tried to free me from the demon, but they couldn't.

"Jesus called us a faithless generation. He asked how much longer he would be among us, and how long he would have to put up with us. Then he said to bring me to him. He walked away from the crowd, and father followed him.

"Most of the crowd were more curious about what had happened on the mountain than about what would happen to me. And they were cowed by Jesus's rebuke. So instead of crowding Jesus, they crowded the three disciples that had come down with Jesus. They pleaded for an explanation of the cloud, the lightning, and the thunder.

"The widow of Nain and her son led me to my father and Jesus. They had stopped next to a small house. That's the last thing that I remember until I woke up. The demon seized me, and I started rolling on the ground, and my mouth foamed.

"Jesus looked at me on the ground and then at my father. He asked how long this had been happening to me. Father said that the way that Jesus asked that question helped him to grasp Jesus's sympathy for us.

"My father told him that it had happened since I was a small boy. He told Jesus about the burnings and the almost-drownings. My father pleaded with Jesus to have mercy on us – to make me well, if he could.

"Jesus was astonished. He said that God could do anything for one who believed.

"Exhaustion brought about by constant sorrow had drained my father's faith. His faith was tiny enough to be lost between the tips of his thumb and forefinger. He said, 'I believe.' His eyes searched the ground when he said that. Then he looked in Jesus's eyes and pleaded, 'Help my unbelief.'

"He did not know it then, but that was a prayer.

"The crowd shifted its attention to us. They came running to where I still foamed from my mouth and writhed on the ground.

"Jesus told the spirit that caused me to be deaf and mute to come out of me, and never to enter me again. I screamed, and I convulsed horribly. After that, I had the stillness and pallor of a corpse.

"My father stared at me, motionless on the ground. Some in the crowd said that I was dead. He heard them say that. He dropped to his knees. He bent from his waist, covered his face with his hands, and he bowed his face to the ground next to my face. He stayed like that for a minute, silent.

"Then Jesus stooped and took my hand. I became aware again. I felt his hand.

"The first thing I heard was the breeze shaking the leaves in nearby trees. Then I heard the caw of a raven. I opened my eyes. I sat up. Someone said, 'Look!'

"My father looked up. His eyes widened. Jesus helped me stand. It was hard because my legs were shaky. My father got to his feet, too. I looked up at my father's face and said, 'Papa.'

"On the way home, we talked about what had happened. Father did most of the talking. For weeks, it wearied me if I talked too long, and it made my throat ache.

"Father told me that he was greatly comforted by the fact that Jesus told the spirit not to enter me again. He said that it was hard enough to believe that the horror was over after it had been part of his life, day-after-day, for five years. He said that if Jesus hadn't said that, he would have dreaded that one day the demon would come back.

"As we walked, I listened to father sing psalms. He listened to me sing, too. He said that my songs were sweet to his ear. He said, 'Your voice is not the same as it was when you could speak before. Of course! You are older now!'

"We got home. Mother wept for joy.

"That day, neighbors came and went. They praised God. But in lonely, late-evening lamp light, mother and father sat across from each other at our table. I sat between them. Father rested his hands on the table in front of him.

"Mother said that what had happened made her think of the prophet Elijah. Especially, she thought of Elijah's contest at Mount Carmel with the prophets of Baal.

"She said, 'Elijah told the people to choose between God and Baal. He said that the prophets of Baal should make an altar, sacrifice a bull on it, and call down fire from their god. Elijah said that he would do that, too. And whichever god sent fire, that was the god the people should follow.

"'The priests of Baal stacked their wood on the altar, killed their bull, and put the bull on the wood. Then they called fire down fire from heaven. They called on their god for hours. They sliced their backs with swords. But nothing happened.

"'Then Elijah cut up a bull, and he put the wood and the sacrifice on the altar. Elijah told the people to soak the altar with four buckets of water. He made them do that three times.

"'Then Elijah prayed. God sent down fire. It consumed the sacrifice. The fire even licked the water from the trench around the altar.'

"Mother said, 'Our own fear and doubts were like the buckets of water that soaked the wood, the sacrifice, and the altar. But this prophet Jesus was un-burdened by our fears and doubts. He called the power of heaven, like Elijah had called down the lightning of God to take Elijah's offering for the sins of the people.'

"Father protested that he had had enough faith to take me to Nain and to Mount Tabor. Mother stretched her arms across the table, pressed her small hands on top of his big hands, and beamed into his face.

"The next day, father and I were sitting under our oak tree. The three men from the north came. We saw them coming when they were far off. When they came close, Father stood and shouted:

> But if you don't wish to serve the Lord, then today choose whom you will serve – the gods that your ancestors served beyond the river, or the gods of the Amorites in whose land you stand!

"Then I stood up. I shouted, 'As for me and my house, we will serve the Lord!' I picked up a rock and threw it at them. It bounced off the Oracle's shoulder. They turned and ran. I chased them for a mile, throwing rocks at their backs.

"Later, when we learned how Jesus's clothes and face had changed on Mount Tabor, we also learned that God had spoken to the disciples who were with him. On Mount Sinai, God gave Moses the Law. On Mount Tabor, God told Peter, John, and James to listen to Jesus.

"My father did listen. In time, he felt called to come here, into Samaria. He traveled here to spread the good news of Jesus Christ – the son of God, the God who heals, the God who raises the dead. This Jesus was crucified, died, and was buried. God brought him up from death and took him up to heaven. He sits at the right hand of God."

The three-dozen bandits continued to listen.

"Father made several trips into this land. The last trip he made he never came back from.

"I am my father's son. I come here in my father's place. You can kill me, but that will get you nothing of lasting worth. Or you can let me baptize you in the name of Jesus Christ, by water and the spirit.

"Then you will have no fear of death, because your resting place will be in heaven with God. Blessed be his name forever. Amen."

2

VESTMENT

John 7:53-8:11

"Ananias died?"

The grey-haired woman looked up from sewing. "We haven't talked about that, have we?"

"Never at length."

"I heard he died soon after the tongues of fire came on the disciples in Jerusalem. His wife Sapphira died on the same day."

"He was with the followers of Jesus?"

"So I heard."

"You must have been glad."

"Not that he died. I wasn't."

"But not sorry, either?"

"No."

The dark-haired woman finished sewing the seam of a linen robe and set it aside. Like the grey woman, she had crescent eyebrows over brown eyes, and a straight nose. Both were good-looking. They could have been mother and daughter, but they were not.

"How young were you?"

"Young. And outwardly unstained."

The dark woman looked at her friend.

The grey woman looked back at her and sighed. "It was costly to lose my reputation." She examined the robe she was sewing. "It's getting dark. Shall we make light?"

The dark woman poured oil into lamps while the grey woman took fire from the oven. They lit the lamps together.

The grey woman picked up the robe she had been sewing, sat in her chair, and continued. "One day Ananias followed me into the small court that we shared with two neighbors. He came into the shop. He was tall, broad-chested, and he had a face like you want royalty to have.

"He and my husband chatted. I retreated to a far corner of the room as they examined clothing we had made. Ananias bought some small things.

"On his next visit, he bought other clothing. I was glad that we'd gained a customer of such good standing.

"His voice had authority, confidence. He impressed me with his choice of clothing. In truth, everything about him impressed me – from his big hands to his grey hair. And his words.

"When he talked to my husband, I studied him from across the room. He was urbane. My husband was – not."

"A young woman's crush."

"Yes, that's true.

"After he had visited less than a handful of times, he said that he would be busy more than usual for a few weeks, and he didn't have time to come to the shop. He said that he knew that my husband had his own business to manage, but perhaps he could send me, his wife, to his home, to take and deliver his orders?

"My husband looked at me, then back at Ananias. He hesitated.

"Then Ananias quickly said that he understood if I could not be spared, and that was too bad, because he would be needing several new garments for himself and his family. Perhaps, he wondered, there was a shop closer to his home that my husband could suggest?

"So I went to his home. When I saw it, I was breathless. It was made from dressed stone, three stories high. The windows and doors were intricately-carved olive wood. The lattices in the windows, too, had tasteful art carved into them. The entry-way led to an inner garden-court with fruit trees and palms.

"I was self-conscious, but it was just business between Ananias and me. The second time I went to his home, he asked after my husband. And he asked for advice about some clothing he wanted. We talked at length. He was charming. But I kept my wits about me.

"The next time, I brought his son's new tunic and robe. I put them in his servant's hands. Then the porter took me to Ananias's roof. I did not understand why the porter was wearing a garment that I had made for Ananias.

"Ananias was sitting on his couch. He seemed to brood. He didn't look up. He asked me if I had brought the garments. I said that I had. He was silent for a time, and then he sighed.

"He stood. He looked in my eyes. He said that he was pondering the book of Qohelet. He wondered about a text in it. He recited the text: 'Who knows what is good in this life, all the days of this valueless life that we pass as shadows? Who can tell us what will come after us under the sun?'

He asked, 'Tamar – what do you think?'

"I hesitated. I said, 'I don't know.'

"'You must have an opinion. It's important to me.'

"'Why?' I searched his face.

"He looked in my eyes and waited. I bit the inside of my lips and looked down. I'm sure that I looked like I was trying to find the tip of my nose with my eyes."

The dark woman tilted her head and smiled at her friend.

"Suddenly, I thought I had the answer." The grey woman shook her head slightly. "I looked in Ananias's eyes. I said, 'A priest!'"

The dark woman ejected a soft laugh.

"Ananias's jaw dropped. But he quickly recovered his composure. For a moment, it seemed to me that he, too, bit the inside of his lips. I clutched my stomach.

"But then he said, 'I'm glad you think so. That's what I think, too. We'll speak of these things later.' His smile was like sunshine on my face.

"I walked home hardly aware of where I was going. I kept rehearsing that short conversation in my mind. I even added to what I had actually said.

"After that, I would come to his home and meet him on the smooth tile floor of his roof. Ananias would speak lines from a psalm or other revered texts. He would ask me what I thought they meant.

"Ananias always seemed full of thought after I spoke. Then he'd tell me his opinion, which always seemed to me wise and good. He made me feel mature, and wise, and – wifely.

"I came to know when Sapphira, his wife, would be gone. In those times I would go to his home without any business. I sat on the floor at his feet as we spoke of holy mysteries. I thought that surely this was from God, to shape my understanding of the Lord with this godly man. When I would walk to his house, I fought with myself whether to hurry, to get there quickly, or to go slowly, for the sake of seemliness and dignity."

The grey-haired woman lapsed into a silence. The dark woman asked, "Is that robe you're making for the tanner's widow?"

"It is."

"What happened with Ananias?"

"One day I went to his house when Sapphira was gone. I called into his house, and Ananias himself called me up to the roof. A servant followed me up the stairway on the right side of the house, but Ananias gave him a stern look, so he turned around and went back down.

"Ananais was sitting. I expected him to speak, as usual, of holy things. But instead he sat and looked at me for a time. Then he said, 'Tamar'.

"I was thrilled, like I'd been summoned for honor out of a great throng. He continued to look at me, and I said *his* name.

"He rose from his seat and kissed me. I stifled a cry. He persisted. He lifted my head-covering. Then he pulled my clothing off over my head."

The two women were quiet for a moment.

The gray woman continued. "After that, his porter wouldn't let me in. There were no new orders.

"I would wait around near his front door. His servants shooed me away like a stray chicken.

"I would look for Ananias in the streets of Jerusalem. If I saw him, I would follow him. Sometimes he or his servant would see me, and his servant would come back to block me from continuing.

"My husband, of course, knew that Ananias no longer bought from us, and that I was morose. I didn't explain, but what had happened wasn't hidden from him.

"One day, I went to draw water, and I heard my name behind me. I turned, and it was Ananias's chief servant. He came up and smiled and said that his master wanted to see me. That was what I yearned to hear. No question or suspicion crossed my mind.

"He handed me a silver coin and told me to meet Ananias at a certain inn on the road into Jerusalem. He told me to give the coin to the innkeeper. I hurried to the inn. On the way, I spent a few copper coins on perfume, a hair pin, and black makeup around my eyes.

"I knew the danger, of course.

"The inn was run-down. The innkeeper seemed to expect me. I gave him the silver coin. He directed me to a room. He brought grapes and figs.

"I sat and waited for about an hour. Then Ananias came. He smiled down at me as he came through the cloth that covered the door. I stood up. He took a grape from the fruit that the innkeeper had brought and put it in my mouth with his fingers.

"I tried to give him a grape, but he took it out of my fingers and tossed it aside. He cupped my chin in his hand and told me to make myself ready. Then he turned and walked out.

"I pulled off my clothes and lay on the bed."

The grey woman looked down.

"Suddenly, men burst through the curtain that covered the door. They grabbed me by my hair and my arms and rushed me outside. They pulled and pushed and carried me kicking, screaming, and pleading into Jerusalem and through its streets. A crowd followed.

"These men were scribes and Pharisees. They were well-dressed. As they hauled me, they jostled with each other to be the ones to grab me. Some slid their hands over my body.

"I was certain that I was going to be stoned to death. I also thought that they were going to rape me. At first, I was too shocked to wonder why they took me into Jerusalem. Stoning always takes place outside city walls.

"While I struggled and screamed, one of the men shouted to the others, '*Abaddon has no covering*!' The others shouted their approval. I knew that verse. I knew its beginning."

The dark woman said, "*Sheol is naked before God.*"

The grey woman looked in her friend's eyes and smiled slightly. "Strangely, it calmed me, a little. I didn't struggle or scream after that. I thought that maybe God would be more merciful to me than these men. But still my heart beat like a bird caught in a snare.

"To my shock and disbelief, they took me into the Temple.

"They manhandled me up the steps to the temple grounds. These irregular steps were made for solemn ascents. In their haste, the men stumbled.

"They manhandled me up through the tunnel that leads to the Court of the Gentiles. In that court, they stood me in front of a man I hadn't seen before. At that time, I didn't know Jesus by sight.

"A strong man gripped my hair from behind. Two others gripped my upper arms. I couldn't cover my body, so I covered my face with my hands. I cried.

"Every pair of eyes but one raked my nakedness.

"They told Jesus what I had done. They asked him what he wanted to do with me. They pointed out that the Law required death by stoning. They demanded his judgment.

"Jesus said nothing. The shouting stopped. I felt their eyes peel away from my nakedness. The men holding my arms let go. The man gripping my hair released his grip.

"I wondered what was happening. I dropped my hands and crossed my arms over my breasts, and I looked at Jesus. He was bent down and making movements with his fingers on the ground, as if writing. He never lifted his eyes to me.

"I looked around; my accusers were studying Jesus.

"The scribes and the Pharisees kept asking him whether I should not be stoned. But they were quieter, more respectful than at first. Then Jesus stood and, looking past me, he said that the person who stoned me should be the one who was himself without sin.

"He said it without apparent judgment on my accusers. He said it as if it were a natural idea, one that my accusers might have come up with if they had stopped to think. And his words lingered after he spoke.

"Then Jesus bent down and kept writing."

The dark-haired woman asked, "What was he writing?"

"I have no idea. Nobody knew. It wasn't ground that you could leave a mark on with your fingers.

"The point wasn't what he was writing. The point was that, whatever he was writing, it took everyone's attention away from me. And the point was his calmness and his focus on something other than the naked woman in front of him.

"There were some muted half-attempts to argue, which Jesus didn't answer. My accusers were embarrassed about themselves. They had lost heart for the debate.

"The crowd dissolved. They didn't look at each other as they left. Not at me, either.

"Jesus stopped writing. He bowed his head for a time. Then he stood up, looked in my eyes. He asked me where my accusers were. I said there were none.

"Then he said that he didn't accuse me, either. And he told me not to sin any more. Those words also lingered, and afterward they continued to linger.

"At that moment, a woman came next to me. She was about the age I am now, and she had a robe. She looked surprised. She asked me if I was Tamar. I said I was.

"She helped me dress. Then she embraced me, and she took me to her home with her arm around me."

"That was my aunt."

"Yes, it was. I never saw Ananias after that. I didn't grieve his passing.

"But I was heart-sick at what they did to Jesus. They were the hard-hearted ones. They were the ones who deserved to die a terrible death, not Jesus. It was impossible to believe."

After the short silence that followed, the dark-haired woman added, "Until it wasn't."

Tamar smiled widely. "Yes, until it wasn't."

She stood and shook out the robe she had just finished. She said, "The tanner's widow will like this."

3

TRADE

Matt 15:21-28; Mark 7:24-30

The two-year-old girl clasped the bony knee of her sitting grandmother. She looked up with wide-eyed delight. Two other girls, seven-and-nine years old, sat on the floor in front of the old woman's slippered feet. A boy, six-years old, sat next to the girls. Outside, a servant drew water from the cistern.

The grandmother grinned at the clinging little girl. She traced her finger down the back of the girl's black hair.

"Grandma, tell us the story!" the boy said.

The children's long-limbed, elegant mother sat in a chair behind the children. She shushed him. She smiled at the smaller, old woman, her mother.

The grandmother pulled the little girl onto her lap and looked into the other children's eyes.

"It was when your mother was as a little younger than you, Sarah," she said, speaking to the oldest child.

"There was laughter and drinking and conversation and food on the roof-patio of my home. I paid for the home and what was in it with the ships I sent to Damascus for wine, to Greece for copper, and to Arabia for lambs, sheep, and goats. My ships brought these back here to Tyre to sell.

"I was telling my guests what I thought was an amusing story. It was about a Jew who had pleaded with me for alms. I said 'This Jew in the street stood in my way. His wife and two children crouched at the side of the street. He asked for money. I told my servant to follow me around him. Then he looked at the olives and goat cheese that my servant carried, and he gestured. Oh! He painted on such a hopeless face! I told him, "It isn't right to take the children's bread and throw it to the dogs!"'

"This caused much amusement among my guests.

"A bejeweled young woman in an embroidered robe, the daughter of a shipbuilder, asked, 'Did you really call them *dogs*?' Then she laughed loudly, showing all of her teeth. The men near her laughed too, and there were several of them.

"A tall young man wearing a purple silk tunic and a red robe, a high official's younger brother, said, 'Beggars! Once you help one, you won't be able to go from one place to another. Every four steps, there'll be another outstretched hand in your face. And you can't stand in one place, because they'll search you out!'

"A third man, my cousin, with a mouthful of cheese, just said, 'Jews!'

"My father cleared his throat, and those around him turned to him. I asked, 'What is it, father?'

"He said, 'I've traded in Judea and Galilee. They were honorable, scrupulous. They were men who dusted their scales.

"He continued, 'We come from Zaraphath. There, a holy man from Israel kept a widow alive in a time of drought. He came to her from his own land. He asked her for water and a piece of bread. She said that she was gathering sticks to cook a meal. She was making the meal from her last morsel of flour and oil. She and her son expected to eat that and die.

"'He told her not to be afraid. He told her to make a meal for him and for her and her son. He promised her that her oil and her flour would last as long as he stayed with her.

"'The holy man stayed with her while the drought lasted. During that time, his word was true.

"'And he made her son live after her son had died.'

"After my father said this, there were snorts from some of my guests.

"Then my father added, 'Holy men still live in the land to the south.'

"This, of course, was shocking talk among people who worshiped Baal and Astarte.

"In ancient times, as now, we imported wheat and honey and other foodstuffs from Israel. We gave them timber. We also provided skilled workers to build their temples and palaces. We taught them how to sail their fleets.

"Jezebel was a queen of Israel. She was the daughter of our King Ethbaal, and she was a missionary. We gave them our god Baal.

"One of my guests, a trader, spoke of rumors of a man from Galilee, a man who performed miracles like the great prophets of Israel in times past. Then, a man who traded in Galilee and Judea, a tall, thin, slightly stooped man with thin grey hair – he said that he had seen this man.

"He said that he had gone to Galilee to see a prophet named Jesus and to hear him preach. He said the preaching was good, and Jesus performed amazing miracles. People were healed of un-curable diseases. Demons were driven out of people.

"When he said *demons*, all talk stopped. My guests looked at me. The speaker looked embarrassed.

"I left my guests and went downstairs, to my daughter, your mother."

The oldest girl asked, "How did you know she had a demon?"

The grandmother answered, "We won't speak of that, dear.

"The affliction had gone on since she was three, and it came and went. It became part of the pattern of my life. I hired people to pray to Baal and Astarte for her. Her nurse was always with her. I bought silver statues for the temple. She did not get better.

"When I went down to your mother's room that evening, her nurse was grimly studying your mother's face. Her nurse didn't take her eyes from your mother as she said, 'There's a change in her.' I sat with the nurse and your mother for half-an-hour, and then I returned to my guests. Some had gone.

"There was more talk of Jesus. He had been seen in the region between Tyre and Sidon, the region that our family came from.

"My guest who had seen him spoke of his teaching – how the poor were blessed and the rich were destined for sorrow. All of my guests were wealthy. Some scoffed, but some listened.

"So did I, especially when my guest spoke of the miracles. My prayers and my gifts to the god and goddess of Tyre had done nothing to help your mother.

"Then there was a shriek from downstairs. It was your mother's nurse. I ran down, and others followed.

"Your mother was at the point of death. I ordered my guests out of my home. I told a servant to summon an exorcist.

"While we waited, your mother went back and forth to the edge of death. The exorcist came and chanted until morning, but nothing changed.

"I paid him and sent him away. Then I told my servants to prepare to go north. We were going to the region of Zaraphath to find Jesus.

"We loaded donkeys with gifts and food. We left as quickly as we could. Along the way, we asked other travelers what they had heard of where the Jewish prophet Jesus was.

"A traveler coming from Zaraphath said that he had seen Jesus up the road. He said that Jesus had gone into a house with his disciples. I ordered my servants to go ahead of me with the donkeys and gifts and to give them to Jesus. I came behind my servants.

"On the way to the house, I imagined Jesus and his followers inspecting the gifts that I had sent ahead. I pictured Jesus rubbing the costly Egyptian linen between his thumb and forefinger. But I worried that he might not know the value of the gifts. My guests had said that he lived simply. I wondered if such luxuries might be strange to him. *No matter*, I thought, *I can explain their value when I arrive.*

"I came to a house and saw one of my servants in front, surrounded by my donkeys. He held their reins and looked at me blankly. But I thought, *Good, the gifts are inside.* I went into the house confident that I would be welcome.

"I came into the room where Jesus and his followers were eating a fragrant stew. My servants stood around the table with their backs to the walls. Their arms were so laden with the gifts for Jesus that some of them could not see in front of them.

"Men were stretching their hands to the middle of the table to dip their bread in the common bowl. These men ignored my servants, except for one disciple. He kept looking at the gifts, then at Jesus, then back at the gifts.

"From that man, I knew which man was Jesus. I walked around the table and stood behind him. I said, 'Sir.'

"He ignored me. Some of the men at the table looked at me, but then they looked at Jesus and returned to eating.

"I stood there for a little while. Then I knelt. I spoke louder. I said, 'Sir!'

"He turned his head and looked at me. I was about to speak, but he turned back to the table.

"I looked up at my servants. My chief servant looked at me and then at the floor. When I caught his eye again, I signaled for him and the other servants to leave.

"When my servants were gone, I bent so that I was on my hands and knees. I pleaded, 'Sir, my daughter is tormented by a demon. Please help me. Please, she is very ill. She'll die if you don't help.'

"Jesus paused. Then he turned and said, 'I was sent to the lost sheep of Israel.' He was not haughty when he said that. If anything, he was sad. He turned his face back to the table.

"He was so close that I could have stretched out my hand and touched him. But it was as if there were a wide chasm between us that I could not cross. In my mind, I shrieked across that chasm, *Then why are you here? Why aren't you where the Jews are?*

"And while I mentally shrieked at him, he stopped eating and looked directly forward, as if a thought had struck him. His disciples stopped eating and looked at him and at me.

"In the silence, I thought of the young Jewish man and his wife and his two children who had pleaded for alms from me. I wanted to give Jesus donkeys loaded with rich gifts. But I wouldn't give that desperate family a coin.

"Then Jesus half-turned his body toward me. He looked in my eyes and said quietly but clearly, 'It isn't right to take the children's bread and cast it to the dogs.' Then he returned to eating.

"That broke me. I was judged, and I was judged right. I groaned and pressed my forehead to the floor."

The little girl on the old woman's lap twisted around and looked up. She touched her grandmother's face. The grandmother took her hand.

"After a few minutes, I stood to leave. As I left, I looked back at Jesus from the door of the room. He did not look at me, but the big man who sat on Jesus's right-side did. As he looked at me, he was drawing his bread-hand back from the common dish. His arm bumped the arm of the disciple next to him, and that made him drop his bread. It hit the edge of the table and fell onto the floor

"When I saw that, a thought came to me. I pleaded with Jesus, 'But even the dogs under the table eat the children's crumbs!'

"Jesus stopped eating. He looked up at me. His face shone. He said, 'O, dear woman, your faith is great. It is as you want.'

"At that hour, your mother was well. There has never been a hint of trouble since.

"I brought the gifts back to Tyre, since Jesus didn't want them. I gave them to the needy."

The oldest granddaughter asked, "Did you give them to the Jewish man and his family?"

The old woman parted her lips, but she immediately resealed them. She looked at the floor in front of her feet. Then she glanced at her daughter.

Her daughter said to the child, "Sarah, grandmother couldn't find them. But she has helped many people like them."

Still looking at the floor, the old woman said, "I sent people to search for them. I learned that they'd been robbed on their way to Tyre. That's all I could find out. Nothing about what had happened to them." She shifted her gaze to the shiny hair of her youngest granddaughter, who was still on her lap, giving attention to her own fingers.

"The time for me to help them had come and gone. One day you'll understand, dears, that that helps me to remember that I didn't earn the Lord Jesus's kindness by anything that I said or did.

"And I have never ceased to worship and serve him since the moment when he healed your mother."

The oldest daughter asked, "Is that why the church meets in your home?"

The old woman acknowledged that this was so. And she said that she had to return there, because the church was meeting that evening.

But first she laid her hands on the heads of each of her grandchildren, and she prayed for their protection, and that each would grow in the grace and blessings of the Lord Jesus. She prayed for the boy to become a man after God's own heart. She prayed for the girls to become women who refreshed the spirit of God. Then she prayed for her daughter, and her daughter prayed for her. Then mother and daughter enlisted the children, and they all prayed for the old woman's son-in-law.

Then she left, with good works behind her and before her.

# 4

ALL

Mark 12:41-44; Luke 21:1-4; Acts 6:8-7:60

A dark, tattered, cotton sheet covered the corpse's nakedness. The sheet went from the bottom of the corpse's rib-cage to the middle of its shins. Lying face up, the corpse stretched the full length of a long table. The long table filled most of the tiny room.

A square, chest-high window streamed afternoon sunlight. Thousands of dust mites swirled in the light. The window made a rectangular light-field on the corpse from the middle of its naked chest to its sheeted upper-thighs.

Dimmer light glowed from the flames of two slipper-shaped olive-oil lamps. They sat on the table next to the corpse's head and feet.

A gaunt old woman barely kept her hips away from the edge of the table by leaning her slightly-stooped back against the wall behind her. She squinted at the streaming light.

The light shone on the back of her hands, with their crisscrossed veins. She carefully pressed down on the flesh of the corpse. She started below the breastbone and inched down the abdomen. Then, with the help of the other, younger woman on the other side of the table, she lifted the torso to almost a sitting position. Then they laid the corpse's torso down again. The old woman grimaced at the faecal smell.

The young woman stepped back from the corpse. She looked down on the unseeing eyes. White slits divided its upper and lower eyelids. The eyelids and the flesh around them were mustard-colored, purple, and black.

The old woman said, "I've done this before. My husband was your brother's age."

When the old woman spoke, the young woman looked up at her. Then the old woman took up a bloody hand and arm and scrubbed them clean. The young woman did the same on her side. They dipped their cloths in a clay jar that was on young woman's side of the table, half-way between the corpse's head and feet. The water took more blood and grime every time they re-wetted their cloths.

The old woman said, "My husband helped build the Temple. He was a stone dresser. He was one of the thousand craftsmen and ten-thousand workers hired by King Herod.

"It would have stirred his spirit to squint into the Temple's face in the morning, when the sun shines on it. He would have woken up glad every morning that he went to build the temple grounds. But he didn't live long."

They moved in tandem toward the top of the table. The young woman bowed her head. The tips of her long, dark hair fell forward and almost touched the motionless face.

The old woman looked at her for half-a-minute. Then she said, "There were times when I seethed with bitterness. I told this to a friend. She listened to my pain for weeks. Finally, I asked her why she wasn't more bitter, since she was a widow, too. Did it pass with time, I wondered?

"She asked me if I felt better when I seethed over my own needs and my own misery and the hard hearts of the well-fed. She asked, *What does it do for your hunger?*

"I admitted that it no longer helped me when I unburdened myself. She asked me what I might do instead. I thought about that. I said that I might watch for God. That is what my sweet, strong mother had taught me. In my pain, I had forgotten."

The young woman straightened up and wiped her brother's cut lips and broken nose, then the rest of the face and the neck. With a cup, she poured water over his hair and scrubbed clotted blood out with her fingers.

Then the old woman placed one of her palms on top of the corpse's head. Her hand touched bone through a deep slice in the scalp. She placed her other palm firmly under the jaw. She pressed the mouth closed, and they bound the broken jaw with a white napkin.

The old woman lifted the sheet and scrubbed down the bruised and broken torso. As she did, she said, "My friend reminded me of the story of Ruth and Naomi. My mother had taught me this story, too. But I had forgotten about it.

"Ruth was a Moabite. Her husband was Naomi's son. Her husband died. Naomi's own husband and her other son died, too.

"So Naomi went from Moab back to her home, Bethlehem. Ruth went with her. Ruth supported herself and Naomi by following reapers in the fields and gathering grain that they left behind.

"There was a rich man, Boaz. He was related to Naomi's dead husband. He noticed Ruth when she gleaned in his fields. He helped her.

"One night, Ruth seduced Boaz on his own threshing floor. She became his wife. She had a son, Obed. Obed was the father of Jesse, and Jesse was the father of King David.

"Of course, you know that story."

The old woman rolled the body on its side to scrub the back.

When the body was face-up again, the two women massaged its hands. After that, they joined the hands on the chest.

The old woman continued to speak as she cleaned the top of the corpse's legs. "It's strange about David and threshing floors, isn't it? His grandfather was conceived on one.

"And when David brought the Ark of God back from the Philistines, he carried it on an ox cart. It should have been carried on poles. The oxen stumbled at the threshing floor of Nacon, and Uzzah stretched out his hand to steady the ark. God struck Uzzah down."

She put a hand under a cold knee to hoist it so that she could scrub under a leg.

"At another time, David sinned, and an angel of God slaughtered 70,000 of our ancestors. The angel stretched his hand over Jerusalem to destroy it. God held the angel back by the threshing floor of Araunah the Jebusite."

She wiped one foot, and the young woman wiped the other.

"David built an altar there. And the place of that alter became the first temple, built by Solomon. That site is the site of the temple we have today."

The women swaddled the corpse's hands and feet in strips of linen. From time to time, they stopped while the old woman spoke and the young woman listened. At those times, the young woman unconsciously touched the arm or head of her brother.

"I found out that it consoled me to pray in the Court of the Women, in front of the Temple. I join in when there is singing.

"One day, I had two tiny copper coins. I sat and looked at them in the palm of my hand. Could they buy a proper meal for Passover, which was coming? They could not. In truth, they would have added little to any Passover meal even if I had joined with others who were poor like I was. The copper coins seemed like two kernels of wheat to feed a wedding party with.

"I remembered better times. I remembered life with my husband when he was building the Temple. Ruth had left her people to care for Naomi. I had left my people so my husband could build the Temple.

"I stood up. As I walked up to the Temple, clasping my two coins, I quietly sang songs that my mother had taught me. One was a song for heaven's help. It went:

> Answer soon, O Lord; my spirit dies.
> Don't hide, or I lie in the common grave.
> Let me hear your love at dawn.
> I trust in you; teach me to walk,
> For I lift my soul to you alone.

"Closer to the Temple, I sang a song of praise:

> Your reign never ceases, your rule never ends.
> Your words are faithful, your deeds are gracious.
> The Lord braces the falling; he straightens the bent.
> All eyes take in the rhythm of your giving.
> Your open hand makes all creatures glad.

"Outside the temple grounds, I immersed myself in one of the pools. Later, I climbed the wide Monumental Stairway on the south side. I went through the Double Gate and up through the right-hand tunnel under the Royal Stoa. Under the roof of this grand portico on the south side of the grounds, I exchanged my two tiny Roman coins for two tinier coins – two perutahs.

"As I turned away, out of the corner of my eye I saw the money-changer mocking me to his neighbor. He thought I didn't see him.

"Among all the people going to the Temple or coming from it, nobody noticed me. Why would they? People notice the lepers who come to be inspected by priests more than they notice an old widow. That's the way it is.

"Then I went around to the east and through the doors into the Court of the Women. Those great doors made me feel small, like the copper coins in my fist.

"From those doors, I could see across the vast Court of the Women, up the stairs, and through the Nicanor Gate. It was mid-afternoon."

The women anointed the body with fragrant oils.

"The high alter was in front of the Temple, to the left. Fragrant smoke from sacrifices rose to God. But, of course, I was going only to the Court of the Women, where the treasury is, to dedicate my copper coins. I tarried for a time. I sat by myself, listening to the music.

"Late in the day, the crowd grew, which was unusual. I decided it was time to leave. I walked to one of the thirteen wooden boxes for gifts to the Temple. I felt foolhardy. I thought, *Why should I give away both coins?* But then I wondered: *What good will only one coin do, either for me or for the Lord?* So I said a little prayer and put my two coins into the box.

"The man who put money in before me gave silver; maybe the one after me gave gold. I gave what I gave. Then I said another prayer and left."

They bound sweet spices to the body with more strips of cloth. They covered the face.

"Something happened. God blessed me after that. People I didn't know started to be kind to me. I don't know why. It was easier to get by.

"Then, the Holy Spirit came on the disciples in Jerusalem, and people flocked to join the followers of Jesus. I was among them because of the kindness they had shown to me.

"That made every difference. Never in my life have people been so generous, so giving. I have little, but I never have too little."

She said quietly, "And that was how I met Stephen, your brother. Among those who made sure that people like me were taken care of, I loved him best. He was so kind, so loving. He was full of the Spirit of Truth. No wonder he spoke out so boldly in the name of our Lord.

"I'm so sorry. He held nothing back." As she said this, her voice broke.

The two women met at the foot of the table, embraced, and wept.

5

MULTITUDES

Matt. 8:23-34; Mar 4:35-5:20; Luke 8:22-39

He knelt like a man praying. A film of water slid over the boulder under his knees and wetted the hem of his outer tunic. He bent and scooped his cupped hands into the stream. Water splashed his scars. In the almost-twenty years since shackles had sliced his wrists, the scars had faded. As he drank, water slightly darkened his beard, which was dominated by grey and white hairs. He stooped for more water.

"Hey! Hey!"

He straightened and turned to see a man of about twenty-two years, who hailed him. The young man slipped and stutter-stepped down the steep bank beside the stream. From the foot of the bank, the younger man walked up to the taller, older man and studied his sun-creased face.

The young man said, "I know who you are!"

The older man blinked. He pushed his shoulders forward to stretch the broad shoulder-muscles below his neck.

"Tell me, friend."

The unblinking young man pointed at the other man's chest. He said, "You're the preacher."

The older man's head snapped back slightly, as if the newcomer had flicked the tip of his nose. Then he smiled. "Yes, that's who I was."

The young man asked, "Which way are you going?"

"North."

"Me, too."

"Shall we go together?"

They walked on the road of crushed stones, wide enough for four men to walk abreast. The older man said, "You must have been a little child when you heard me preach."

The young man said, "I never heard you preach. My father pointed you out and said who you were."

"Ah. What did he say?"

The young man looked away. "I've heard of Jesus. I know he cast out demons. My father knew only some of your story."

"Are you a believer? Was he?"

The young man's lips pressed against each other and his brows pressed toward each other. He said, "I have doubts."

"Tell me about that."

The young man grimaced again. His dark eyes looked to the middle-distance. "My father –" he started. The older, taller man waited for him to go on. But the young man only said, "If Jesus is God, and he came to make the world right, I don't know why people suffer like they do."

They walked at a calm pace for about one-hundred feet. The one-time preacher asked, "Have you asked a believer who has suffered why they believe?"

The young man considered the question. "Do you talk about your story?"

"Do you want to hear it?"

"Yes."

A raven stared at them from the middle of the road like a surly, squat, wide-stanced sentry. As they came up to it, it turned and flew north, going ahead of them.

The older man said, "I was maybe four-or-five years younger than you, and I was zealous. I fasted every week. I sat at the feet of the teachers in the synagogue of Gadara.

"I studied their teaching to try to make myself perfect. I added to my knowledge every day. It was a privilege to study under my teachers, and I cherish what I learned from them.

"My father was pious, but he worried that one day I would be old and poor and shunned by respectable men. He believed in work, that it was ordained by heaven. He said that it was his calling, and everyone's, and mine, too. I didn't share his reverence for everyday life and ordinary occupations.

"He encouraged me to court a certain girl. She was the daughter of a man who traded in wool, like my father. She was a fine girl. My father took me to meet her father. Like my own family, he and his family were among the Jewish minority in the Decapolis.

"As we talked, her father spoke of the Law of Moses. I corrected him. He was gracious. He smiled and made a slight nod, as if to acknowledge the weight of my words. Then he glanced at my father.

"That began the long spectacle of an older man speaking and a younger man schooling him. He made another point, and another, as if he were trying to edge ahead of me with his knowledge. You would have thought that once, just by good luck, he might have said something right. But I didn't see it that way.

"Part of me knew that I was overstepping, and that I should stop. The other part of me thought that heaven had handed me a ripe chance to show my learning to my father.

"As the back-and-forth between our host and me went on, his speech became terse and his eyes sharpened. My mortified father thanked him for receiving us into his home, and we left. We walked home without speaking.

"I hadn't shown respect or restraint. I should have gone to the girl's father and asked for his forgiveness. That's what my father told me to do. People had a high opinion of my father. If I had shown contrition, that and my father's high merit might have given me back the goodwill of my would-be father-in-law. Instead, I prayed for him. The marriage didn't take place.

"I was fine with that. My future would have started with that marriage, a future like my father's life – buying and selling wool, caring for a family. I didn't want that future. I treasured a secret hope to become a teacher of the Law. And not just a teacher, but a great teacher with a following in synagogues throughout the Decapolis, or even in Judea.

"My father and I had different pole stars, and one day we lost each other. My father again chastised me about my duty to make a life in the world apart from my studies, with career and family. I didn't argue, but I chafed at what he said, and he knew it. Then I left for the synagogue.

"Once there, I read from the Torah. Later that day, I made some remarks that others praised. So I left the synagogue high in my own mind.

"I came outside with a teacher and some of my friends. My father was waiting for me at the door of the synagogue. He berated me in front of them. That wasn't his nature, but I suppose he had reached the end of his patience.

"He berated me for neglecting my duty to marry and have children. He berated me for neglecting my duty to take up his occupation. But mainly he berated me for my failure to honor the Law that I always studied, because I didn't obey my parents. He kept saying that, in different ways, over and over, as if to smother my religiosity under his words.

"His speech impressed my friends and my teacher. They took his side.

"I was red-faced and stunned. And I was angry at my father. In my anger, I shouted things at him that I can't repeat today without feeling shame. If I'd taken time to think, I'd never have said those things. The people from the synagogue gaped with amazement.

"It was a scandal. My shame from what I said was worse than my shame from what my father said.

"I couldn't go into the synagogue after that. I was lucky to escape violence. I was shunned by my friends. Even my Greek neighbors were appalled.

"My loneliness accused me. It came in like a tide and took me away from Gadara. I had no plan, but I headed south toward Jerusalem. I left at night.

"I crossed the Jordan River above the Dead Sea. I rested in the shade of a tamarisk tree near Jericho. A big man joined me there. He spat as he talked. He held up his hand to show me his missing finger.

"He was companionable. He asked my name and where I was from. He asked me where I was going and why. I was careful in what I told him. But anyone could see that I was rootless, and I told him about my studies in Gadara. He had bread and a small skin of wine, which he shared. He asked me what I thought of the Roman domination of Judea.

"He belonged to of a band of men who had plans to drive the Romans out. He invited me to stay in a camp in the Judean hill country with himself and other like-minded men. I followed him for company and food, and for lack of other options. But I got caught up in the calling.

"My companions were ruthless, but they practiced piety. They spilled blood, but then they cleansed themselves under the rites of the Law.

"One day, our leader and a number of us went into a town. We shouted out to people to stop and listen. We called to them to get their friends to hear the good news about the coming end of Roman domination. Our leader touted our success at harassing the hated Romans.

"He called for people to stop paying taxes to the emperor. He called it *tribute*. He said that tribute was idolatry, especially since it was paid with coins bearing the emperor's own raised image.

"It was foolish to be there and to do that. But we were rash, grandiose young men. We had sworn, if need be, to die for the kingdom of heaven.

"I was a lookout. Nothing seemed unusual. People came and went.

"Then I heard people chanting. I listened, and it was a psalm. Its beauty mesmerized me.

"I walked toward the chanting. But the sound of it mixed with a growing cataract of footfalls and the clang of metal on metal. I came to the cross-street, and a squad of Roman soldiers charged out from it. They pivoted toward the marketplace. Each soldier seemed like a giant. I became words of the psalm that I'd been hearing. At that moment, if I could have, I would have fled like a bird to the mountains.

"The Roman soldiers burst into the marketplace like a torrent. There was screaming and yelling. My friends had no chance.

"The Romans crucified the ones that they didn't kill right away. I hid while the soldiers patrolled the town. After that, I came out of hiding.

"The road down from the town took me past my friends. They hung on both sides of the road. Some of them pushed themselves up by their heels, which were nailed on each side of the vertical post of the cross. Then, their chests could expand enough to breathe. After a time, they grew tired and bent their legs. With their legs bent, their lungs struggled against the lack of air. Those still living were exhausted.

"My friend whom I met under the tamarisk tree outside Jericho had suffered a deep cut to his leg when the Romans took him. He lacked strength to raise himself up. He was already dead.

"I puked. As I squatted in the road, a passing man put his hand on the back of my neck, and he told me – too loud, I thought – that he too vomited the first time he saw men crucified. I retreated back to the town.

"A few days later, I walked out of town past the place where my friends hung. I kept to the center of the road, looking up to the left and right. Blow flies swarmed the corpses. Ravens pecked at my friends' eyes and picked maggots."

The older man stopped talking while a donkey and rider trotted past them.

"I got to Gadara, and my father took me back. No: I should say that he welcomed me back. My brothers were less welcoming.

"Even though Judea was far away, most of the time I was afraid to leave the house. My father spoke gently to me. He said that if the Romans came, we would face them together."

The older man brushed a wasp from his sleeve.

"One night, I dreamed an absurd dream. It was crazy, but it oppressed me.

"I was in the Jerusalem Temple, in the Court of the Priests. I was between the tables where the animals are slaughtered and the altar where their smoke rises to God. I was walking toward the front doors of the Temple. A white-bearded man dressed in a blue robe and a vest covered with twelve different kinds of jewels was there. He rushed out of the Temple toward me. He stopped me in front of the Temple.

"He was furious. He said that I was born to lead an army against the Romans, but at the moment that I cursed my father, I had nullified hundreds of years of prophecy. He said that I was an offense to heaven, and that I would die like my friends in Judea. He ordered me away.

"In my dream, I fled through the Shushan Gate in the east wall of the temple grounds. The sun was setting. I was in the Kidron Valley beneath the Temple Mount. Tombs were everywhere. And every time I took a step, my foot landed on a grave. I tried to get away from the tombs and graves before darkness came, but I couldn't. I couldn't get to the Mount of Olives, but I couldn't go back to the Temple, either. That was because a man with a sword stood in the way. His face was hidden.

"I woke up with my heart pounding. I calmed down, but then I sat up in my bed and fretted about the dream until morning.

"In my home, I became suspicious of my family. No matter what happened, I turned it into proof that they planned to give me over to the Romans to be crucified.

"I made assumptions that couldn't be made, but I couldn't help making them. If someone was glad, I believed that they were glad because they knew I would die soon. If they were sad, I assumed that they knew that my end had been delayed.

"I didn't know that they knew that I was suspicious of them. But one day my youngest brother slammed his hand down on the table during a meal. He stood and yelled down at me, 'Stop staring at us like enemies! You don't have to say anything, but then just eat!'

"Everybody was still and quiet. Then my father dipped his bread in the dish, as if nothing had happened.

"After that, I obsessed on the idea that my youngest brother had a demon. As time went on, I thought that everyone in my family was demonic. That scared me, but at least I knew why my own family had turned against me.

"I fled. I stayed with a friend's family.

"But the same thing happened there. In my mind, all of them became demonic enemies. I went to another house, but I fled in less than an hour. After that, no doors were open to me in Gadara.

"But it didn't matter, because I decided that every household in Gadara was a nest of demons. Even the beggars had power over me, and I was afraid of them. Like them, I slept in the streets. I always tried to find a place away from people.

"My father and brothers would hunt for me. I went the other way whenever I saw them coming, because I was afraid.

"One day, I stopped to look at a goose, just to think of something that didn't oppress me. It spread its wings, it lowered its head, it walked at me, and it hissed. I thought, 'Even nature abhors me here.' So I fled north.

"As a solution, that failed. I came to Raphana's gate. There was a man there who I never saw before. He smiled, but his eyes were filled with hatred.

"Inside the city walls of Raphana, I discovered that it was the same with everybody. It was the same in Hippos. I figured it would be like that anywhere I went. I gave up on cities.

"During this time, I came to believe my weird dream. The fact that I seemed to be the object of a vast conspiracy of demons and men made it more and more plausible that I was as important as my dream said.

"I walked from Hippos down to the Sea of Galilee. I found tombs. Obviously nobody lived there, and there I felt safe from demons.

"As I walked among the tombs, a firm voice told me that heaven had seen my suffering and had compassion. The voice said that I could come under heaven's protection and fulfill my mission against Rome, but I had to vow perfect obedience. I did. I would have promised anything.

"The voice commanded me to throw my clothes into the sea. I balked. But the voice said that if I couldn't do this little thing, I couldn't do great things, hard things. The voice sternly reminded me of my vow, and it warned me that if I failed at that moment, I would get no other chance. So I cast my clothes into the sea.

"A short time passed, and the voice said to retrieve the clothes. I tried, but the tide had taken them, and I couldn't swim."

A hare darted up the road away from the two men.

"News of me reached Gadara. People from home started coming for me. When I saw numbers of people coming, I would run away, usually to the mountains. But hunger brought me back. The people of Hippos left food near the tombs.

"Sometimes big men that my father hired would come. If I was asleep, they would sneak up, rush, and pounce. At first, it was just a few men. I would shake them off like twigs and bruise and bloody them. I had the strength of many in my body.

"A story caught on in Hippos that I was Samson, alive again. In fact, I had long hair like Samson's, not short hair like yours, and like mine is now, and like it was before my time at the tombs.

"But I wasn't Samson. He was a great hero. But maybe, in a rough-hewn way, my time at the tombs was like Samson's time in captivity. I'll say how in a moment.

"The people who came to take me got smarter. A whole crowd would come. If they caught me asleep, I couldn't shake them off because they were heavy and I was groggy. Then they would shackled me, but I would break the shackles and chains and run off.

"I would go without sleep for days and nights as I watched for the men my father sent, even if they hadn't come for many months. When I couldn't keep my eyes open or my head up, I would pace among the tombs. That would stave off sleep for a little while longer. I even harmed myself with stones, just so the pain would keep me alert.

"I had no idea that they intended me good. In my mind, they were coming to give me to the Romans for crucifixion. I believed that they wanted me dead because I was the Messiah, and when I was gone, nobody would be left who could resist the Romans and the demons. With my death, the league of Satan and Rome would prevail, and I would be flicked into hell.

"That thought was always in my mind. I dreaded hell and imagined its misery. I even imagined demons in hell taunting me as their biggest prize and most ridiculous captive, because my sin had made them triumphant.

"I craved mercy from heaven.

"That was one way that I was like Samson in his captivity: I shared his craving for mercy. The other was this: we both received it.

"One night, toward morning, there was wind. It came in waves and blew out over the water. It worried me. I sensed demonic forces in it.

"The wind grew steady and strong. It pelted me with pebbles and twigs.

"I thought that the windstorm was about me. In my mind, it foretold that the king of demons was gathering forces offshore. Then he would come to where I was.

"I had lost greatness before I knew that I had it. But now my soul went weak because I was about to lose the little pleasure that I could still enjoy. As long as I was alive, I could study the busy-ness of living things in inches of ground. On some days, clouds made me think of glorious temples in heaven. That thought was a green shoot in thirsty earth. Others would have the thing that I had lost.

"I could steal moments like those from my grief. My life was lived in fright, but that was better than starting the future that frightened me.

"Suddenly, the wind died. Morning light and warmth rolled across the land from behind me, and nature began to uncurl.

"I stood looking out from the top of the slope next to the shore. I heard oars stroking the water inside the offshore mist. Boats appeared. I thought that these boats held the army of Satan. But there were fewer boats than I had expected, and I was surprised that they were so small.

"Then I heard a voice from nowhere: 'You are strong. Fight.' So I waited for the king of demons.

"The boats touched the shore, and people started getting out. I had expected warlike men. But they looked ordinary.

I supposed that there was a clever plan behind this. Perhaps they wanted to catch me unaware.

"One of them stepped toward me. I knew that he was the leader. I rushed down at him. As I did, the other men froze and stared in fright. That gave me hope.

"Jesus didn't flinch.

"As I ran, an army of angels with their feet in the mist appeared behind Jesus. Each angel was an armored colossus holding a sword. Seeing them, I knew I couldn't win. I fell down on my hands and knees in front of Jesus.

"He said, 'Unclean spirit, leave him!' I didn't understand.

"I shouted that he was Jesus Son of the Most High God. My own words surprised me. I didn't know how I knew that. And I had determined that I myself was the Messiah.

"In the presence of Jesus the Christ, I was petrified. I was appalled at my hubris in believing that I was the Messiah. I was shocked at the harm that I had intended against him.

"Jesus told me to say my name. Until he gave me that command, I had thought that the demons that tormented me were in the world. But suddenly, I knew that wasn't true. I knew that the demons were in me. I said, 'I am Legion. There are many of us.' Jesus didn't act surprised.

"There was a herd of pigs nearby. I pleaded, 'Please, send us into the pigs.' I would live in the bodies of pigs, but I at least I would live. That would keep me out of hell for a little while longer. But I didn't expect that grace; it was too great.

"Jesus looked at the pigs, he looked back at me, and he gave permission. And suddenly I was in my right mind. I was sitting on the ground, looking up at him.

"I didn't see the pigs stampede into the sea, but later I saw drowned pigs that the tide pressed against the shore. Swineherds ran along the shore, looked out to sea, and stomped their feet into the ground. Briefly, the stink was as famous as my deliverance from the demons.

"I talked to the men with Jesus, and I talked to Jesus. Mostly, Jesus asked me questions. I was overjoyed as I talked. When I answered his questions, my mind became clearer.

"Before the boats came that morning, I had forgotten the feeling of peace. But with Jesus, I forgot what it was like to be afraid."

The young man said, "After that, you were famous for your teaching."

"I was known in some places, yes. After I came home, I started telling people my story. First, I told it to my family. Then I told friends. People were amazed, but they couldn't argue against the fact that I was pitiable before, and I came back restored. More and more people wanted to hear. I started talking to larger and larger groups.

"After a while, I started to add elements from the Prophets and the Psalms to my own story.

"I was pleased with the multitudes that came to hear me. I meditated on my own words. I heard reports of other teachers, and I compared my following to theirs.

"In time, I started losing popularity to others. I resented that. As I preached, I looked at the people who were listening. I felt like I had to will them toward heaven by the strength of my passion for the Lord. But, really, it was passion for the passion of the people gathered to hear me.

"So I appealed to local ill-will against Rome. I did that in a way that I thought would escape hostile notice. But people who knew what I was saying knew what I was saying. People started to hear me again, but it wasn't the same as before."

The young man said, "And then you fled from the governor's palace so fast that you left behind your cloak, your staff, your purse, and your sandals. Then you never spoke out again, right?"

"I was in the home of a leader in a mid-sized town. He honored me with a banquet. He asked me to make a new teaching and to give it for the first time in his town. I said I would.

"During the banquet, a squat, clean-shaven man made me uneasy. Any time I made any slight reference to Rome, I looked at him, and he quickly looked away. He wasn't friendly.

"He left suddenly, and I was anxious. My host was speaking, but I got up to follow the man out the door. I found him outside. He was urinating.

"After the banquet, I tried to create a new teaching, but I couldn't. It was like building without stones.

"I prayed, which was a habit that had leeched away. It felt like trespassing. I gave up.

"I thought of the crowds. I brooded on the fact that I had largely lost them, except for the occasional man, like my host, who remembered my glory. I resented the loss of that glory. I remembered better times.

"I thought that maybe I should go back to the origins of my fame. And I pictured Jesus telling me to say my name. And I remembered the discovery that the demons were in me.

"That memory was like a shooting star — small, brief, clear, and bright. So I prayed again. And I asked God to show me my fault. My thoughts drifted, and then I thought of Jesus, who restored me to freedom, and his disciples, who treated me with dignity and kindness, and who clothed me. Jesus had told me: 'Go home and tell your friends what mercy God has shown to you.' That memory was another shooting star.

"So I prayed, 'You're right, Lord. For as long as you choose not to hear my prayers, I can't complain. Only restore me to your grace at the right time.' I went to bed. After a while, I felt peace, like the peace I felt with Jesus by the Sea of Galilee.

"Since then, I haven't preached. Preaching is a good thing, the good of which God doesn't want from me. I leave it to those who are called to it. I honor good preachers, good teachers. I won't do it myself."

The young man considered this. Then he said, "But I heard that Jesus told you to preach in the Decapolis about the mercy that God showed to you."

"That's what I said when my teaching was popular. But Jesus said only to tell my friends. That's what I do. I share the mercy that heaven has shown me with friends, like you."

"You felt far from God when you were low, and also when you were high in the world."

The tall man smiled and nodded. "It seemed that way. Seemed."

"Why you? Why did demons enter you? Was it punishment because you cursed your father?"

"People wonder that. And they wonder, *Why so many*? I used to think that it was because of my sin. That's the natural thing to think. What I did was terrible. But other people have done worse things, and they lead normal lives. They even prosper.

"I've stopped wondering. It could have been my sin. It could have been both my sin and my zeal. The zeal was sincere, but it was equally a means to raise myself up, to draw others to me.

"Or maybe things go on in heaven and earth that touch us that we don't know about. Or maybe it happened so that today I could tell you this story.

"Having an answer seems less urgent now than it used to. All I know is that when I had no hope, I fell on my hands and knees in front of Jesus the Messiah. From that moment, everything changed.

"I saw the pig carcasses, and it was like I could see with my own eyes that the filth in me was driven out and dead."

In the distance, a man gathered herbs from his garden.

"I'm a wool merchant. I'm not poor and not rich, but I have enough to share with people who have less than I do.

"I'm married. My wife is dear to me, and I would lay down my life for her. I have a quiver full of sons and daughters. Before they were born, I would not have believed that I could love anyone as much as I love each of them.

"And I belong to Jesus the Christ. There are a lot of us."

The young man asked. "So, is that what you tell people if they ask you why people suffer?"

The older man tilted his head slightly to one side, and then he looked at the young man. He asked, "Do you know the book of Job?"

"I know the story from a Jewish neighbor."

"It starts with a description of the man Job. It describes Job's virtue. So the teller of that story starts with a cheat."

"A cheat?"

"The cheat is like the game with walnut shells and a chickpea. The cheater hides the chickpea and never puts it under the shell. So as careful as you are to watch him shuffle the walnut shells, you never pick the shell that hides the chickpea. The chickpea was never there.

"That's the book of Job. For most of the story, you think it's about Job's virtue and why a virtuous man like Job suffers. But at the end you find out that it's not about Job. It's about God. It's about trust."

"Ah. So, we are free to sin because righteousness does not matter?"

"No! By no means! Right choices matter very much. But they matter because they please God, grace our neighbor, and open our eyes.

"Look. I went to school as a young man. May the Lord bless my teachers for all time. But the synagogue in Gadara wasn't the only school I went to. I went to Job's school, too. It taught me not to look to myself. It taught me to look to the Lord."

The older man glanced at the young man.

"There's another thing about Job. Among all that he lost, he lost his children, too. He lost all of them in one day." The older man looked at the far hills.

He said, "Of my seven sons and three daughters, I lost two daughters and one son." A tear wetted his cheek. His beard took the tear like furrowed earth takes a drop of rain.

He said, "I know God because I've met his son, my Lord. I know he loves my children more than I do, if that's possible. When I see my lost little daughters again, they will be more beautiful than before. And my little son will be even more perfect than he was." More tears fell like grace.

"But when my little ones died, that understanding was not quick, easy, or sure."

The tall clouds ahead of them were bright on one side. The road ended where another road crossed it.

"So, young man. What do you think about all of that?"

"They're thoughts to chew slowly."

"I go west."

"I'm going east."

"What's your name, friend?"

"I'm Kyros."

"Kyros, I'm Baruch. Go with God, Kyros."

"Also you."

Each man went his way. Kyros walked east at a thoughtful pace. Baruch strode west with light steps.

6

Pluck

MATT. 9:18-26; MARK 5:21-43; LUKE 8:40-56

"Your father will be missed," the older woman said to the young woman next to her. The older woman had black hair despite her forty-some years. Her shoulders were straight. Her face was seasoned but handsome. Her eyes were half-closed but quick. Her body was taught, and her legs were sinewy from many miles walked on Roman-built roads. She sat straight-backed and cross-legged on the grass.

The other woman hugged her knees to her chest and rested her chin on her knees. She was half the older woman's age. Her dark brows lifted to a peak and then sloped softly down to the sides, like the wings of the seagulls that she followed with her eyes.

The women sat at the tip of a finger of land that stretched into the Sea of Galilee. A few feet in front of them, little waves slapped sand.

The older woman waited for the younger one to speak. When she didn't, the older woman continued.

"Your father and I knew each other before, but our lives parted. His soared. Mine plunged. He was Jarius, the synagogue official. I was an outcasts. I lived among outcasts like me."

She turned her head and looked at the younger woman. "What do you want to know about us?" she asked.

The young woman tilted her head back. Then she turned her face to the older woman. She asked, "What happened that day? And what led up to it? Papa told me the story, but I want to hear it from you. Everything."

The older woman looked out to sea. "Everything," she echoed. She nodded once.

The younger woman returned to tracking the gulls with her eyes. She said, "Papa told me that what Jesus did for you made him remember that Jesus didn't help him because my papa was important."

Still looking forward, the older woman nodded again. She smiled, but not so much that it was obvious that she was smiling. "I'm glad that I had that effect."

She continued, "My mother and father were modestly prosperous in a prosperous place, and I was their only child. I became the young bride of a man who owned property there and nearby. The lines of my life fell in pleasing places.

"My husband and I were close to your father and mother. Your mother and I grew even closer when we found out that we would have our first babies near in time.

"You were born, and they were overjoyed.

"But by then my life had turned bitter. In the last months of my expectancy, I wept by the graves of my mother, my father, and my husband. Then my baby boy was born.

"This is what should have happened after he was born. I would have been unclean for seven days. On the eighth day, my tiny baby boy would have been lifted out of my arms and taken to be circumcised. In that ritual, he would have gained the blessings and protections of the covenant that God made with our ancestor Abraham forty generations ago.

"Then he would have been given back to me. He would have been hungry, and I would have given my breast to his lips. That touch would have shared with me the blessing and protection of his circumcision. I would have become clean on the eighth day.

"All this you know.

"Thirty-three days later, my purification would have been complete. Then, forty days in all after my baby boy was born, I would have taken a young lamb and a small bird to the altar. A priest would have slaughtered the lamb for a burnt offering and the bird for a sin offering.

"Daughters of course aren't circumcised. So when a daughter is born, purification takes twice as long.

"You know that, too.

"Now, all of that didn't happen. My baby was born alive, but when he was born, he couldn't breathe. In minutes he was dead. The midwife gave him to me, and I cradled his naked, blue body and his thin, curly, black hair against my breasts. Then I buried him.

"I was already sick with grief. But then the last thing happened. After the birth and death of my baby, the blood did not stop. I bled as women bleed, but it never ended.

"So if people touched me, or if they touched something that I'd touched, then they too were unclean. That was bad for them. It could have been catastrophic for the city. The great danger was that my un-cleanness would spread from person to person, until the chain of defiled persons reached the synagogue and polluted it.

"So I had to be apart from other people, from everybody I knew. That was especially true of your parents. Your father was an official in the synagogue. Defilement might have gone, arrow-straight, from me, through him, to the synagogue."

The older woman looked at feathers floating in the water.

"I became part of a colony of outcasts under trees by a stream. That's where I lived when people started calling me Mary the Dweller by the Dark River, or just Mary Dark River.

"Most of the people in my new community had skin eruptions. Some of them, like me, were there all the time. Some were there for a short time, and then they went back to their towns and villages. Some came and went, came and went. Some died there.

"At first, I stayed to myself. I was a hermit among outcasts. Even when I started to talk to others, I was too angry to make friends.

"But in time, I grew tired of beating the air with my fury. I started to look around.

"In time, I could see how equal we were in our exile. Being rich didn't save you from becoming unclean; being good didn't save you, either. The worst and the poorest among us weren't more cursed, at least in our uncleanness. The best or the richest weren't more blessed.

"We know from history that King Uzziah had leprosy until the day that he died, while his son ruled Judah. Naaman commanded the Aramean army. The prophet Elisha told him to wash in the river. Naaman's had a skin disease, but he was cured at the river.

"These were subjects of earnest conversation in our colony. We longed for a prophet like Elisha.

"Life by the river had its consolations. The sound of rushing water was soothing day and night. And tent-living by the river conserved my small wealth.

"I could have used my money and property to make myself comfortable, as much as I could.

"But comfort wouldn't have been enough. Someone in our colony would leave and not come back. They would walk away to show themselves to the priest, to be declared clean and restored to the community. I would watch them take the path by the stream until they were out of sight.

"I had a friend. She was old. People came to her for advice. I don't remember what name her parents gave her. We called her Miriam. She had leprosy.

"She would let me complain. I would say, 'When someone leaves this place, in my mind I walk with them. In my mind, we walk and talk about all of the things that we'll be doing soon – things that we can't do here.

"'Miriam, I want to marry and start over. I want to hold a little baby in my arms. I want to love him and watch him grow into a brave, good man. I want the love of a kind husband.

"'I want to bargain for vegetables, to hear children playing games, to laugh with women in their homes.'

"Miriam was from Capernaum, like me. She admitted, 'I miss that life, too, Mary. Women who do those things live a hallowed life.'

"I said, 'It's taking place close by, Miriam. But no matter how long we walk, we can't get to it.'

"I devoted my wealth, what there was of it, to cure my bleeding. A physician would have a cure. I would hear about him and I would seek him out. I gave him money.

"Maybe some of those physicians were sincere. Some were not. Most of them calibrated their fees to my desperation. I gave up my fortune piece by piece. For every piece I gave away, I got back only a week or a month of hope.

"One doctor sold me a tiny amount of copper dust. He said it came from the snake that Moses lifted up the desert, so that the Israelites could be healed by looking at it. I said to Miriam, 'Isn't that amazing? What does a snake represent but evil and sin? How could looking at a thing of sin, lifted up, cure anything?'

"Miriam shrugged. She said, 'Moses was a great man who towers over great men. God did wondrous things through him.'

"I believed in the copper dust. That was because, at first, this physician acted like his copper dust was too valuable to sell to a nobody like me. When it didn't work, I begged him, and he sold me a greater amount.

"And then, one day, in addition to everything else I had lost, I was out of money. That stopped my pilgrimages to find salvation in medicine."

Mary stood and stepped off the grass onto the narrow strip of sand. She took seven short, barefoot steps into the sea. She kept her robe out of the water by holding its fringe in her hands. With the water half-way up her calves, she turned around and continued.

"There's a psalm. The psalm says that the psalmist's enemies taunted him as with a wound, while they said, 'Where is your God?' But I told Miriam, 'I have a real wound. For twelve years the wound itself has said, "Where is your God?"'

"Then a newcomer brought news to our colony. He told us, 'A man healed the Centurion's servant by the power of God.' That was the Centurion who had built a new synagogue in Capernaum.

"This was exciting news. I quickly found Miriam and shared with her what the man had said. She thought. Then she said, 'This man of God isn't going to come our dark bend of the stream. We'd have to go to him.

"'But if we waited for him on some byway, Mary, what are the chances that he will pass by us?

"'Can we look for him in Capernaum?' She laughed softly and shook her head. 'But people loathe us there.'

"She was right. The psalm that I was speaking of – it speaks of going with the throng to the house of God. But throngs were exactly what we had to avoid. In a jostling throng, I would pollute many people.

"And, from what we heard, Jesus was always at the center of a throng.

"Miriam said, 'Would this man even want you and me to approach him? He's holy. That's where his power comes from. That's his strength. He would never want my disease or your dark water' – that was the other meaning of my name – 'to pollute his holiness, to stain his clean-ness.'

"Of course, she was right. Clearly, he would not.

"So that was that. And that's how it would have been if it weren't for the song of the waters. It came to me in my sleep.

"I dreamed that I drifted above the Jordan River. But the river was not calm; it thundered. The sound of the waters thrilled me like angels' voices. I floated above the waters from the gushing pool at Mount Hermon to the shore of Capernaum. People on the shore were eating and drinking. They laughed and shouted at me to join the feast. But I kept on going.

"I woke up praying.

"I shared my hope with everybody in the colony. I said that I felt in my spirit that the Lord was telling me to go and be healed.

"Miriam confronted me. She said, 'We are lost sheep, Mary. We are lost to everyone from our lives before we came here. Don't bring a curse on yourself. Don't let your selfishness put all of the other sheep in the flock at risk.'

"She said, 'Mary, listen. People would stone you. That's likely to happen if you go to Capernaum. Stay here and live, Mary. I don't want to lose my friend.'

"I loved Miriam, but the dream moved me. Others quietly helped me make a plan. First, I had to get into Capernaum. In the end, I borrowed a man's cloak. He said, 'After Jesus cleanses you, ask Jesus to touch the cloak. Then when I get it back, I'll be healed, too. Prophets have that power.'

"The cowl of the cloak would hide my face. My plan was to kneel at Jesus's feet and plead with him to heal me. Then I could walk away healed and later show myself to a priest.

"When sundown came, I sneaked out of the colony. It took a couple of hours to stumble along the paths to Capernaum by moonlight. I slept under a tree outside of the city.

"The next morning, in Capernaum, I didn't draw any glances. Many strangers came to see Jesus. I was only another unknown outsider.

"I found Jesus, but I couldn't get the courage to push my way to him through the crowd. There were people in the crowd that I knew. I dreaded discovery and quick death. That dread paralysed me.

"Instead I floated back and forth behind the crowd. I didn't see any chance to dart in.

"The next morning, early, people were starting to gather to hear Jesus teach. The crowd was loose, and I walked forward through the empty spaces between people. I picked my way through the crowd like you might pick your way across a wide steam one stone at a time.

"I was almost in front of Jesus. But before I got to him, a man with a committee of elders walked in front of me. He kneeled at Jesus's feet and pleaded with him. It was your father, Jarius."

Mary came out of the water and sat next the young woman.

"He said that his only daughter – you – you were at the point of death. Your father pleaded with Jesus to come to his house and save your life.

"And off they went: Jesus, Jarius, and the throng. As they went along, more people joined.

"In my mind, your father was Jacob, and I was Esau: he had stolen my blessing. And Esau couldn't have been angrier than I was then. My anger drove me.

"My friend by the river had said that he wanted Jesus to touch his cloak so that he would be healed when he got it back. If Jesus's touch was so potent, I figured, touching his clothes would heal me. I would be healed invisibly.

"An eagle diving is not more dedicated to her prey than I was to Jesus. I must have squeezed past many people to get to him, but I have no memory of that. I only remember being close enough to see the warp and woof of his cloak.

"And then I tripped. I fell just behind him. I looked up, and my face was almost in the fringe of his cloak. I had just a moment before he walked out of reach.

"So I plunged my scraped and bleeding hand forward and plucked at the fringe. My finger and thumb barely pinched the blue cord around its bottom.

"But at the moment of that pinch, I felt a surge of vitality from top to toe. At that moment, I knew that I was healed. I knew that even as people stepped around me and over me.

"Then the crowd stopped, because Jesus had stopped. He said that someone had touched him. I could hear my own heart pounding. I stayed on the ground with my head down.

"His disciples tried to tell him that everyone was crowding him, including themselves. They said that a touch meant nothing. They seemed baffled. I hoped that Jesus would listen to them.

"But Jesus said that, No, power had gone out from him. I felt like a thief caught in a burning house.

"People near me looked down at me. Jesus and his disciples joined the people already looking my way. The crowd separated and made a path between Jesus and me.

"I crawled forward on my hands and knees. I couldn't have stood anyway. My legs were too shaky.

"Kneeling in front of Jesus, I said, 'Master, it was me.' I told him what I'd done. I couldn't look up.

Then Jesus lifted my cowl back from my head. I looked into his face. He was joyful. He said that my faith had made me free. That was the morning's second healing."

The older woman gazed up at far clouds that spread like a vast plain.

"But there was fury in the crowd. They were shocked that an unclean person like me had pushed by them to get to Jesus, polluting them as I pushed by. Of course.

"Jesus seemed to look far away. But with my sudden healing, my confidence surged, and a memory surged with it. I remembered the copper powder that I had brought from the physician.

"I stood and I spoke to the crowd. I said, 'Moses raised up a brazen snake! People looked on it, and they were healed! Behold this man!' I stretched my right arm toward Jesus. That was the third healing.

"The fury vanished. There were *amens* and *hallelujahs*. People who had known me long years before came up and greeted me. That was the fourth healing.

"Then everyone followed Jesus and your father to your father's house. Jesus was inside for a time. Your father and your mother and you came out, but they didn't say what had happened. Your father was hugging you in his arms.

"You were eating a piece of bread and looking at all the people around your house. You had a half-sleepy, half-surprised look on your face. After that, when I saw you together, your father often had his arms around you.

"You were healed of your sickness, and your father and your mother were each healed of their fear. Seven healings that day – a good number.

"Surprisingly, the people of Capernaum saw Jesus act with the power of God, but most of them didn't know the meaning of the things that Jesus did. Some did, like your father.

"But those who didn't – I can't judge them. Because, who knows? If I hadn't spent twelve years by the river, maybe my comfort and happiness would have made me blind, too.

"I had wanted to start over with a family, but instead I spent the next year following Jesus. There were other women who also followed him. In fact, there were other women who followed him named Mary. I was the least of those with that name.

"I saw Jesus labor for his father's kingdom. I saw him walk into danger. I also saw him go off alone to pray. He would come back refreshed, full of zeal.

"That was then. Now I minister in his name. I lay hands on the sick.

"But what I do most is to reach out to the wretched, to outcasts. In his name, I offer them hope.

"I can't do anything on my own. The thing I want them to do, I do too. To this day, I pluck at Jesus's robe. That is, I pray.

"I praise God – for things that I've heard about, things I've learned about, things he's done for me. I thank him in everything.

"I pray for others. I rarely tell them I've prayed for them.

"I pray to know what God wants, and for his will to be done.

"I ask for a pure heart, a clean conscience, and thoughts that please God. I pray to love him more, to know him better. I pray to be able to delight in him. He answers prayers like that.

"I pray to understand scripture.

"I confess my sins or ask him to show me the ones I don't know about.

"I sing hymns. I say prayers that I've learned, I sing verses of psalms, or I pray freely. Sometimes I pray without words. Sometimes I sit and wait. Silence is a part of prayer.

"I pray walking, working, sitting, lying down, and kneeling. I pray alone or with other people. When I'm alone, I usually start on my knees. It reminds me of who I am and who he is.

"If I wake in the middle of the night, I pray until I go to sleep.

"When I wake up in the morning, I ask the Lord how I may live that day for the praise of his glory. I try to call on Jesus's name through the day. Before I go to sleep at night, I ask the Lord how I have lived for him that day, and how I should have but didn't.

"Sometimes I ask him what to pray, or how. Sometimes I confess that I am weary of prayer. I have yet to shock him. My weakness is his strength.

"Long ago, I touched Jesus. If he'd been ordinary, my touch would have defiled him. Instead, it made me clean. I still touch him, and he still takes my sins away. Every day, I hope that a little of my un-cleanness falls away because I've reached out to Jesus."

The younger woman stretched her legs out in front of her. Then she rested her head on Mary's shoulder. Mary stretched her arm around the young woman. They sat in silence. Mary's lips moved, but she didn't speak. Gulls coasted above the sea.

7

GIANT

Luke 19:1-10

"I opened my eyes in the half-awake light of dawn. The word *Nothing* floated from my lips. It vanished as if it had been set upon by an invisible quarrel of sparrows.

"I sat up and dropped my thick calves over the edge of my bed. My bare toes did not quite touch the tile floor.

"I gazed around at my familiar surroundings, but I seemed not to be part of them. I patted my hands together carefully several times while I stared dumbly at them. The touch of hand on hand and the slight slapping sound lifted my soul back into my body and reattached me to the world. I massaged the sides of my face through the grey-and-black hairs of my beard. Then I stood and dressed."

He was describing his younger self. His hair was now white.

"I wondered where this apart-feeling had come from. It could not be from God, I thought. I was no idolater. I knew that idolaters take the qualities of what they worship. You can't wake idols or make them rouse themselves. They are shiny outside and dull inside, and they have no breath. I knew this. But I was no idolater. I was a son of Abraham.

"I scooped a handful of coins into my belt-purse. A four-drachma coin slipped from my hand, rapped the tile floor, and wobbled behind a bench. I got down on my hands and knees and put the side of my face to the cold tiles. When I saw the coin, I stretched my right hand forward to seize it. Still kneeling, I straightened my back and peered at the coin. I tapped it twice on the edge of the bench."

He set a basin on the floor in front of the first man in a row of seated men. The man sat on a stool. The speaker kneeled in front of the man.

"I came to my pleasant garden-court at the center of my house. My gangly son was counting silver in the flat of his hand. He glanced at me, closed his long fingers over the coins, and left the garden without speaking. I did not remember giving my son those coins.

"My wife came into the garden. I asked her about our son's money. She continued across the garden without glancing at me. She said, 'He's all-business, like his father.'

"To my mind, my wife's beauty did me great credit."

He cupped his hands and poured water over the feet of the man in front of him. He wiped the man's feet with his towel. The man had no sandals because he was a debt slave.

"I was a chief tax-collector in Jericho. Jericho was a center for tax-collection, like Caesarea and Capernaum.

"As a chief-tax collector, I paid a fixed sum of money to the procurator for the privilege of gathering taxes. Anything I gathered over that amount was my profit.

"From my tax-gathering privilege, I parceled out pieces to my deputies. I made my profit from them.

"Not everyone was skilled in this work. The work could make you rich, but the stomach of a scrupulous tax-gatherer groaned for food.

"There was a golden mean. Perfect balance made people cross the street to avoid you, but it did not provoke tax riots.

"And if people in the street hated me, what did that matter? I was high enough that, if I wanted to, I could insult almost anyone, and their anger could not reach me.

"I hoped to rise higher. I had been summoned to the Roman procurator. His messenger would not say why. The procurator was at that moment in Jerusalem. The summons was for early in the week after the Sabbath."

He had now washed the feet of three men. He came to a fourth man, who tucked his feet under his chair. He turned his face away from the former chief tax collector, who bowed his head, reddened slightly, and slid to the next man.

He continued, "My youngest deputy was also my best one. Alexis's lightly-bearded face, almost Roman in its cleanness, and his outwardly-humble affect – these belied his predatory cunning. He could insinuate himself into the confidence of the wariest merchant. Then the merchant would speak freely. Alexis would listen patiently and then alertly cross-examine him. He delighted in exacting large sums without actually using a knife to pry open the merchant's coin box, which my other deputies sometimes did.

"I loved Alexis. I confided things to him that I told no-one else: political things and gossip that I heard, even about the procurator and his household.

"I was baffled by Alexis's recent aloofness. But I thought he would come to himself after this moodiness passed."

The man whose feet he was then washing was old, had lived a hard life, and had painful bone spurs. He washed this old man's feet with particular gentleness.

"My father gave me a good start with a good education and a good name. But his fortune collapsed when he was about my age in the time I'm talking about. At the end of his life, he was happy to have a son who took care of him as well as I did. He prayed for me every day. I was glad of his prayers, but my wealth was the rock that I had set my feet on."

His towel was now too damp to dry with. He got a new towel. He threw the old water from his basin through the open door into the street, and he poured fresh water from a large jug. Then he continued.

"I wondered that day why it was so hard to find my deputies. One by one, I caught up with most of them. They all seemed sullen and grudging. I was amazed and peeved. They seemed suddenly to have forgotten the income they had from the positions I had granted them.

"There was a cure for that. I resolved to confer with Alexis. Alexis could be counted on for shrewd advice. I thought also that he might know who the ringleader was behind this conspiracy of disrespect. I supposed that Alexis could help me select one or two deputies to dismiss. That would bring the others to heel.

"But I had to be judicious; I had selected my deputies mindful of their political connections.

"At the end of the day, business done, I went home, ate well, drank well, and slept."

The speaker dried the callused feet of a man who had no sandals because he was in mourning.

"The sense of nothingness returned before sun-up. This time, it took longer for me to regain my sense of place among my surroundings.

"After dawn, I went to the synagogue. I sat up front as a young man read from the book of the prophet Amos.

"Many of you grew up in the Hebrew tradition, but many of you did not. Amos was a prophet who prophesied many generations after the northern kingdom of Israel split away from the southern kingdom of Judah. Amos came from Judah and prophesied against Israel.

"He denied that he was a prophet. He said he was only a herdsman and a man who cultivated sycamore trees and trimmed them.

"In the time of Amos, the king of Israel was Jeroboam. Jeroboam worshiped foreign gods. His temple-city was Bethel. God sent Amos to that city.

"This is what the young man read from the book of Amos:

> 'They hate him who rebukes at the gate,
> And they abhor him who speaks uprightly.
> Therefore, since you step on the poor,
> And you take levies of grain from them,
> You've built your marvelous houses,
> But you won't live in them.
> You've planted your pleasant vineyards,
> But you won't drink wine from them.

And:

> For thus says the Lord to the house of Israel:
> Seek me, and you shall live.
> But don't seek Bethel, don't go into Gilgal,
> And don't pass into Beersheba,
> For Gilgal shall go into captivity,
> And Bethel shall come to nothing.

"When the young man finished reading from the book of Amos, an older man went forward to speak. He was tall and broad-faced, with short white hair. He spoke with easy gravity.

"He spoke of history. He reminded us of a prophet before Amos. That prophet and Amos were much alike. Both came from the southern kingdom, Judah. Both prophesied north of Judah, in Bethel. Both prophesied in the time of a king named Jeroboam. Amos prophesied in the time of the second Jeroboam. The other prophet prophesied in the time of the first Jeroboam.

"The first Jeroboam invited that first prophet to share his table, but the prophet shunned this royal feast. He said that God had commanded him not to eat nor to drink in Israel, but only to prophesy in Bethel and go back to Judah.

"An old man in Bethel saddled his donkey and chased after the prophet from Judah. He soon found him resting under an oak.

"The old man said that he too was a prophet. This was true. He said that God wanted the Judean prophet to eat and drink with him. This was not true.

"At the old prophet's table, God told the old prophet that the prophet from Judah would not come to his ancestral tomb. This was because he had dined and drank in Israel. After eating, the prophet from Judah got back on his donkey for the short journey back to Judah.

"Before he got there, a lion killed him. The lion stood by and did not tear the prophet's corpse. It did not kill the dead prophet's donkey, either, even though the donkey stayed next to the prophet's body.

"The old prophet found the slain prophet. He buried him in the old prophet's own tomb.

"That morning, the white-haired speaker said that it wasn't the eating or the drinking, as such, that had doomed the prophet from Judah. It was his wish to be celebrated.

He sidestepped that error with King Jeroboam of Israel. He failed at the invitation of the old prophet.

"I was unnerved. Amos condemned crooked men, and I was a crook among men. Amos warned that God would judge.

"And the prophet that the older man spoke of that morning – look at him! He was revered even generations later. But God struck him down. I wondered what such a ruthless God would do to a lesser, worse man like me.

"All the events from my life suddenly marshaled themselves into order. They lined up like a long row of judges. Each judge issued a single judgment: my life was self-serving and meaningless, and it always had been.

"In my heart, I prayed to God to forgive me for a wasted life. I admitted to God that I was adrift. I left the synagogue perplexed."

The man who's feet he was wiping was a small man with small feet, like himself.

"I might have regained my footing after I got back to my normal routine. But I heard people shouting. I heard 'Jesus is coming!' I knew Jesus was a prophet.

People were running in one direction. I got caught up in the excitement and forgot my perplexity. I ran after the people who were running. I had to pump my legs hard to keep up. My sandals clack-clacked on the street as I ran. That sound got lost as I came close to the on-coming hub of the shouting. I slowed because the crowd was thick.

"I could not see around the men who stood between Jesus and me. When I tried to squeeze to the front, people would look behind them. They would see who I was, and they would press together to make sure that I didn't get through.

"I saw that there was a sycamore tree up the street. I ran to it and climbed into its branches.

"From that height, I saw Jesus. Delighted people were thronging around him and praising God. I had never seen such joy in a crowd.

"I hung directly above the street, about the height of two tall men. Jesus came under me, stopped, and looked up at me. The crowd was focused on him, so of course they followed his gaze up into the branches over his head.

"The roar died down. In fact, the crowd became quiet. Then somebody laughed.

"Hanging there in the silence, I looked down at Jesus. I felt exposed. I recalled how troubled my heart had been as I came out of the synagogue. I expected Jesus to flay me, and for all who heard him to be delighted. I felt dread for the soon-to-come humiliation.

"And then he said my name. I don't know if someone in the crowd had said it, or if he just knew it. He said, 'Zacchaeus, hurry up! Come down! For I must stay at your house today!'

"Dismay rippled through the crowd. They were shocked that Jesus had lifted up the filching hand that dipped into everyone's coin box. Especially since that filching hand fed Rome, with its ponderous, marble jaws and sepulchral hunger.

"I slid down the tree-trunk. People grudgingly opened a path for me to Jesus. I was more than elated. I was euphoric.

"I told Jesus that I would give half of my wealth to the poor. And I said that if I had cheated anyone, I would return what I had wrongfully taken. I promised to do this to the greatest amount Moses demanded: four-fold restitution. I said *if* I had cheated anybody. But I knew that I would be left with little wealth after I made good my vow.

"That didn't matter. My joy soared.

"Jesus put his hand on my head. To people looking on, this emphasized my small size. He said to me, 'Today salvation has come to this man's house, because he too is a son of Abraham.'"

Zacchaeus was lifting the foot of an old, bent-backed man who was also from Jericho. The old man barked a laugh. Zacchaeus grinned back at him.

"I wonder how many people that day got Jesus's sly joke. The book of the prophet Amos spoke of the Amorites. Amos described them as tall as cedars, strong as oaks. Our ancestors were terrified of them. The Amorites had lived in the territory around Jericho.

"Jesus had put his hand on my head and said, 'This is a son of Abraham!' He was saying, 'This little man is no giant, no Amorite! He is one of us!'

"In these times, the Romans are our Amorites. We fear them like our forebears feared the giants of their time. Jesus proclaimed me a Hebrew, not a Roman.

"Then he said that he had come to seek out and save what was lost.

"Jesus stayed with me. Many important people came to my home, but I opened it to anyone who wanted to come. Jesus spoke to us, and he ate with us. He asked us about ourselves. My wife and my son listened to him. My life turned around, and theirs did, too.

"There was one sullen person among my guests that day. It was my beloved Alexis. But after a time, Judas Iscariot found him. They went outside together. When I glanced up the street, they were speaking with their heads together.

"That day, I started to fulfill my vow to give away my wealth.

"But when Jesus left for Jerusalem, I went too.

"Everything I saw would be too much to tell. But I will always remember the shouting crowds on the Mount of

Olives. They cast their precious cloaks in front of Jesus for his colt to tread on.

"Yet Jesus wept.

"His sadness became anger when he saw the money-changers. He turned over their tables and chased them off the temple grounds."

"There was a man name Bartimaeus with us when Jesus drove out the money-changers. Barteimaeus had been blind, but then he could see. He said that if he were still blind, he still would have felt the fury and the fear. It was as if a lion were loose in the Temple.

"I sucked in my breath later when the Pharisees asked Jesus whether it was right to pay taxes to Rome. Of all people, I knew how much taxes were hated. If he had said *Yes*, he would have lost the crowd. But if he had said *No*, he would have been seized for sedition and killed.

"But Jesus asked for a coin. Then he asked whose image was on that coin. Of course, Roman coins bear the image of the Roman emperor.

"My Hebrew brothers understand that anything that bears a human image is an idol. An idol is an abomination. But we humans are made God's image. That bespeaks our value to God.

"So Jesus said to give to the emperor what is the emperor's and to God what is God's. His answer rebuked the Pharisees. It pointed out that their minds were fixed on something abominable, like Roman coins, instead of on something of true worth.

"Then the Sadducees asked Jesus a bleak question about a man who married a woman and died before she could bear him a child. The man had six brothers. Each in turn married her, as ordered by Moses. This law insures that a brother's line will continue, because the living brother gives his dead brother's wife a child that bears the dead brother's name.

"Each brother died childless, every last one.

"The Sadducees do not believe in the resurrection of the dead. So they asked Jesus who the woman's husband would be in the resurrection.

"The image of a woman surrounded in heaven by her seven husbands was meant to be hilarious. It had obscene implications. Listeners sniggered. The Sadducees' faces had expressions that ranged from grinning glee to hawkish triumph. But their triumph was short lived.

"Just like Jesus turned over the tables of the money-changer, he overturned the victory of the Sadducees. He supplied a better image than the image of seven men standing around their shared wife.

"It was an image of men and women not married nor marrying, but, after the resurrection, transformed into immortal angels and children of God.

"But Jesus was not finished with the Sadducees. Jesus reminded them that God came to Moses at the burning bush. He reminded them that, there, God said that he was the God of Abraham, the God of Isaac, and the God of Jacob. Then Jesus said this: God is not the God of the dead but of the living, because, to God, Abraham, Isaac, and Jacob are alive.

"Again, my Hebrew brothers understand. God and death oppose each other. God is the holiest of the holy, and death is defilement. Under our Law, anyone who so much as touches a corpse is unclean. Even after a victorious battle, warriors are not welcomed back into the un-defiled community. They have touched death on the battlefield. They go through a ritual of cleansing before they rejoin the community.

"Jesus had put the Sadducees in a hard place. They could not deny the authority of scripture. But to have disputed what Jesus said, to have claimed that God was God of the dead, the Sadducees would have had to claim that God was defiled. They would not say that, because they did not want to be chased from the temple grounds and stoned.

"So Jesus cut down these giants. One lawyer was more clever. He said, 'Teacher, you have spoken well.'

"I would have stayed longer in Jerusalem. I even thought that in the blessed company of Jesus, maybe I didn't need to give away so much of my wealth. But through a disciple I was told me to return to Jericho and fulfill my vow.

"Later, I wondered how a crowd that had greeted Jesus so joyfully had later raged for his crucifixion. There are many reasons for this, and God ordained all of them. One of them was a report that spread about Jesus's feast at the house of a notorious sinner. That sinner was me.

"Shrewd men used that story skillfully to turn the crowd. They publicized my sins and sullied Jesus with them. They covered up my repentance. It is well that I was not there.

"In the meantime, I continued to make good my vow.

"And when I met with the Roman procurator, we talked about Jesus. We spoke at length. At the end, he confided that he had planned to put me in prison. He had heard evil reports about me that touched him personally. But recently he had heard good reports about me, he said. He praised my shrewdness.

"Jesus favored me by staying at my house. And Jericho suddenly knew me as the man who was giving half his wealth to the poor. Jesus saved me."

He stood from washing the feet of the last man.

"Quarrels have cracked our community. We have been bitter and hard-hearted. I am with the guilty.

"Please forgive me. My wife also wants forgiveness. She asked for it yesterday when she washed the feet of your wives and sisters."

He walked across the room and stood half-in and half-out of the door to the outside. He poured out the basin-water. He said, "If any of you are in my debt, that debt is gone."

8

THIRST

John 4:4-42

"Father, he shouldn't have spoken to a Samaritan woman."

Her lips barely moved as she whispered her prayer. They moved invisibly in the darkness.

"In my maidenhood and middle age, passing men craned their heads to study my profile. They hoped I would look back at them.

"So I took him completely wrong. When he asked for a *drink*, I thought he meant – something indecent.

"And I was resentful. After all – a stranger? And a Jew? At Jacob's well?

"The Jews had their temple in Jerusalem. We had worshipped at our temple on Mount Gerizim. Then the Jews marched their army against us and tore it down. That was generations ago, but our bitterness was green.

"And there, at the base of the mountain where our meeting-place with God had been demolished, at Jacob's well – there, of all places, this Jewish stranger approached me."

An iron door's rusty groan occupied the hall outside her prison cell. She paused to mourn any ghost entombed in that place of grief.

"But I was alone. Nobody else was around in the heat of the day. So I answered carefully. I said, 'You are a Jew, and you ask me, a Samaritan woman, for a *drink*?'

"He looked at me thoughtfully. Then he said, gently, 'If you knew who I was, you would have asked me for a drink, and I would have given you living water.'

"And, Father, I thought that when he talked about giving me a drink he meant the same as when he asked *me* for a drink. I thought that he was a man being a man, and that he was boasting about his manliness. His flowery talk of *living water* reminded me that some men esteem their romantic desirability higher than others.

"But I thought that he was saying more than just that.

"You know, Father, that the land around Sychar has many springs. I supposed that he noticed that I went to a well at noon instead of to a spring in the morning. After all, a spring is alive; it has water that gushes up and makes pools. But I had to lift the well-water from below by my strength. I supposed that he guessed why I was pulling my heavy bucket up hand-over-hand in the heat of the day.

"I thought that his talk about *living water* meant that he knew what kind of a woman I was. I was a woman who went to a little-used well at a bad time to avoid other women. I didn't want to hear them lash me with their gossip spoken loud enough for me to hear.

"I supposed that that made him feel free to say what he said – or what I thought he said. I supposed that that made him think that I might be willing.

"And I supposed, too, that he was putting me in my place.

"Those suppositions said more about me than about him, of course. And outwardly, he seemed respectful, not like the kind of man who rips your worth and then tries to take you cheaply.

"So he put me off-balance. He seemed just outside of my comprehension.

"But I gave it back to him. I pretended not to understand. I said, 'Sir! You don't have a bucket, and the well is deep!' That was a little boasting of my own.

"It was also spittle at his feet. I was stung by – by what I *thought* he implied.

"But, really, I was who I was. I'd been no wall. I'd been a door that opened for men who knocked.

"You know that I've never been meek. So I also said, 'Are you greater than our ancestor Jacob, who dug this well, and drank from it with his sons and his flocks?' I thought that if I were very, very crude, I could wrench away his appetite. Then he would leave me alone. I blush to remember.

"Jesus gestured to the well. He said that anyone who drank that water would be thirsty again. But that if they drank his water, then they would never be thirsty again. He said it would be a spring that gushed up in them, gushing up to eternal life.

"I was amazed. Here was a man of apparent subtlety, but he would not be put off! He was making the same kind of boast as before! And also I wondered, *This talk of 'eternal life': is he proposing marriage, or is this man's mind overheated?*

"I was becoming uneasy. But I was who I was, Father: deep with strategies to draw men to me, and to push men away.

"So, I half-pretended not to understand. But, to appease him, I also half-pretended to agree. But, as much as I implied that I *did* understand, I suggested that men tired me more than they pleased me.

"I said that I wanted such water, because I didn't like to come to the well day after day. That was true, in fact.

"He sensed my unease. He looked down as if he were in conversation with himself. Of course, it was not with himself, as you know.

"Then he looked at me and invited me to go, to bring back my husband.

"I preferred that direction of the conversation. It put me at ease. But I said that I had no husband.

"He said that I was right, that I had had five husbands, and the man I was with was not my husband.

"And that for a moment took my speech away."

She reached through a gap in her rags and touched her side. Where her ribs were, her body felt like it had been furrowed.

"Forgive me, Father. Until that moment, I had thought that he was coming on to me. But after he told me about my past, then, in the time it takes a drop of water to fall from a jug to the ground, I knew what he had been saying.

"I was amazed. The Jews had marched an army against us. That army had wrecked our meeting-place with God, on Mount Gerizim. But at the foot of that ancient meeting-place, a messenger of God had come. And he was a Jew.

"So I raised the ancient contention between Jews and Samaritans. I said, 'Sir, I can see you are a prophet. Our ancestors worshipped on this mountain, but the Jews say that people must worship in Jerusalem.'

This question was a test. I wanted to know if he was going to approve his people's atrocity against the temple of my people. I wanted to know if he would say that God could be worshipped only where we were not welcome – in Jerusalem. His answer would tell me whether he was a prophet sent by God to us, or if he was just a holy curiosity on his way to somewhere else.

"He said that a new time was coming, a time when people would worship neither in Jerusalem nor on this mountain.

"He said that we Samaritans did not know God; the Jews did. He said that salvation would come from the Jews. *How*, I wondered?

"He said that the time was coming, and that the time was now, when people would worship in spirit and in truth. He said that God sought people to worship him that way. He said that God is spirit, and that people must worship him in spirit and truth.

"His talk about worship in spirit and in truth made me feel uneasy again.

"But he called you *the Father*, and that intimate term attracted me. And so did the idea that we need no temple on Gerizim, and no temple is needed in Jerusalem: buildings are not the locus of worship.

"Father, when he spoke of meeting you in our spirits, this was a new thing. I thought of what I had heard. I said 'I know that the Messiah is coming. He will do something new.'

"Then he said, 'I am he.'"

She paused. She drew her tongue away from the roof of her mouth. Tiny shards of dry phlegm came away with it.

"I knew by then that he was a prophet. But it was hard at that moment to see him as the Messiah. He had no sword, he had no crown, and there he was: alone, on foot, in the pass that led from Jerusalem to Galilee.

"I studied him as we spoke. I wondered, could the Messiah be greater, wiser, stronger-in-soul than this man? He was more than his words, Father.

"But his words were good. He said that I'd been searching for the face of God all of my life, but that I didn't know where to look, so I searched in places where I wouldn't find him.

"My first husband had fields and servants, and Jesus said that I'd married him because his wealth represented to me the power of God.

"But then my first husband died. I married my second husband because he was beautiful. Jesus told me that I had thought that I'd found the beauty of God in my second husband's face. Unfortunately, the beauty of God was not in his soul.

"Jesus said that I married my third husband because he knew so much. To me, my third husband's intelligence was godlike.

"He had studied Jewish holy scrolls and the writings of other religions. As you know, we Samaritans have the books of Moses, but not other Jewish books like the Psalms and the Prophets.

"My third husband would tell me about the prophet Isaiah. He told me that Isaiah saw God on his throne, and that God's robe stretched down from heaven, and its hem filled the temple in Jerusalem. I had been in awe. It was from my third husband that I learned of the coming Messiah, who I met that day by Jacob's well.

"But that knowledge had competed with other knowledge. Until I met Jesus, I didn't know how to value one tradition over another. I worshipped what I didn't know. Jesus was right.

"My fourth husband came from a long-ago noble family. Jesus said that I'd married him for prestige, and that my husband's prestige stood in the place of acceptance by you.

"Then Jesus said that I'd married my fifth husband because I was lonely, and in that marriage I'd sought the consolation and love of God. But I didn't find it in that marriage.

"And then Jesus said that I'd taken to bed with a married man because I was afraid. I knew that one day I would die, and when I was with my young lover I was able to forget that.

"He asked me about Jacob's well, when the well stopped giving water. I said that it usually lost its water in late May. He said that I knew that it was almost that time for me. Truly, it *was* almost that time for me, and I did know that. He said that my young lover was my hope for renewal, but that I wasn't renewed by him. He was right about that, too.

"Then his disciples came. I left my bucket with them and went into the city.

"I went to the city to tell the people there to hear this man who had told me all about my life. But I didn't say that he was the Messiah. If I'd said that, they wouldn't have believed me. But I invited them to see for themselves. Instead of provoking an argument, I provoked curiosity.

"He stayed among us for two days.

There was a moan from a far-away cell. Photini prayed for the sufferer.

Then she said, "It was right, Father, that Jesus came to us at Jacob's well. Our ancestor Jacob had dug this well in a land of many springs, so that he did not have to fight other herders over those springs. The well made peace. And at that well Jesus made peace between you, our Father, and us.

"When I learned of Golgotha, I grieved. But after a time, Golgotha made our meeting at the foot of Mount Gerizim mean so much more.

"As you know, Father, our ancestor Abraham obediently offered his son as a sacrifice to you, until your angel stayed his hand. Our traditions says that this happened on Gerizim. When we learned of the crucifixion of Jesus, we

Samaritans of Sychar – maybe we understood it before others did.

"And the footfalls of our ancestors drew patterns in the sand of the Sinai Desert as they followed Moses. Then, Joshua led them across the Jordan River into this land, Canaan. There were military victories.

"Then, some of Israel's tribes stood on Mount Gerizim, and the others stood on Mount Ebal. They faced each other across the strip between Gerizim and Ebal. The tribe that you, Father, made holy – the Levites spoke curses and blessings. The tribes on Gerizim received for the people the blessings; the tribes on Ebal received the curses.

"At Golgotha, everyone who lives, ever lived, and ever will live – we were all Gerizim. Jesus was Ebal. I thank Jesus for his love that made him take the curses.

"Thank you, Father, for letting me meet Jesus at that well, where peace was made – between Jacob and his neighbours, between my people and you.

"And between you and me. Everything that Jesus said about me was true. And it changed everything about me.

"I had sought power in my first marriage. I only learned what power was when I learned that you had raised Jesus from the grave and had given him the seat of power at your right hand.

"I had sought your beauty in my second marriage. But I stopped looking for your beauty in men as men. And as often as my thoughts turned from men, or from seeking my own pleasure, I looked up and saw your beauty in the sky.

"In time I learned to see your beauty in persons who sought your face, and in the needy. I helped them, as I would have if they were Jesus. And I prayed for them, that they might become giants. And they prayed for me, that I might be a giant, too.

"That was so valuable when I was put in prison, here in Rome. I do not see sky. At first, I found your beauty in other prisoners.

"But now I have no companions, so I've learned to see your beauty in the faces of my captors.

"The official who pronounced my death sentence said that he didn't care about my teachings. He said he hated my immorality.

"That baffled me. You know how flawed I am. You know my flaws better than I do. But by the lights of the world, I have lived nearly a blameless life since I met Jesus.

"But the man who condemned me spoke harshly of old cults. He spoke of their unspeakable practices. He spoke of Jesus's followers as if we did those accursed things. And he blamed us for the six days of fire that burned almost every part of Rome.

"I spoke against this, but he waived me away. The soldiers hauled me out of the chamber as I tried to speak up for my Savior and for your followers. And here I am.

"But there was a glimmer of you in him. I saw it in his hatred of immoral deeds. It was in his wish for a moral world, as he understood morality. It was only strange that he found depravity where it wasn't.

"Also, Father, Jesus took our sins into his body as he died, because a house divided against itself cannot stand. We could not become perfect. So that our house would not be divided, your son became sinful. So, Father, what sin in what man fails to make me think of your son Jesus?

"I hoped for wisdom and knowledge in my third marriage. I've found it in taking up my cross and following you. I learned that the less I wanted from the world, the better I could see what you were doing, and the better I was able to join you in that. I found wisdom in your will. Thank you, Father.

"I wanted prestige in my fourth marriage. But I discovered that when I cared about the opinion of mere men, that made a wall between you and me. I learned to strive to please you instead of men.

"In my fifth marriage, I married because I was lonely.

"Father, I'm so glad that you have not left me to die alone."

A far door clanged open. Light from torches glowed down the hall. A man wailed. But he stopped wailing when the soldiers had passed his cell, because then he knew that they had not come for him.

Photini listened to the soldiers speak in low tones. Their voices grew more distinct as they came near her cell. She heard the words *piss* and *shit*. The glow from the torches increased.

She prayed quickly. "Father, thank you for leading me to meet Jesus. Because of that meeting, I have lived for the spirit, not for the flesh; to teach the truth, not to hide from it. Thank you for letting me bear witness to your glory. That has been my joy.

"Bless my sons. Bless my sisters. Bless your church.

"Please cover my many sins. Thank you for your grace. If you are willing, you can welcome me into life with you forever.

"Father, before I started praying, I was very fearful. Now I'm not much afraid."

She felt love within her. That love welled up and overwhelmed her. It drowned every need, ache, and anxiety.

The door swung open on its iron hinges. Three soldiers held torches. The light flooded Photini's tiny cell. The three other soldiers reached in, grabbed her, and pulled her into the hall.

They did not need so many soldiers. She had no strength.

A soldier spat on her, and others struck her. They hated her because she was a woman, a weakling, an outsider, and a lawbreaker.

As they took her away, she felt pity for them. Her heart yearned for them to know what she knew.

9

PITY

Matt. 22:34-40; Mark 12:28-34; Luke 10:25-37

The door opened, causing the oil lamps to flicker. A thin man stepped across the threshold and stood just inside the doorway of the inn. Dust of Galilee came in with him.

He tugged off his tattered turban. He rubbed his right hand back and forth over his scalp. His beard was wispy. By the customs of the time and place, his bare scalp and almost-hairless chin made him look like a middle-aged man in deep mourning, a ritually-shaved man recently healed of a defiling disease, or a Nazarite who had fulfilled his oath.

His robe and cloak were of good quality when new. Now they had patches.

Eight steps away, at a small table against the far wall, two friends were sitting across from each other. They peered over at the newcomer and nodded to him. He nodded back.

The innkeeper came into the room and closed the door behind the newcomer.

After brief haggling, the newcomer dropped a few coins into the innkeeper's hand. Then he sat against the wall by the door, facing the two friends. He stretched his legs on the floor in front of him. He moaned softly as he bent forward and kneaded his calves.

The two friends resumed their conversation. Both were tall, white-haired men. One had a thick beard. His broad shoulders hinted at the athleticism of his youth.

The other man was slender. His hair was fuller than his friend's, but his beard was more modest. The tops of their foreheads almost touched as they whispered. Sometimes, one or the other would thump the table with the heel of his hand as he made a point.

After a minute, the newcomer asked, "Are those your donkeys under the tree?"

The thick-bearded man paused his conversation and answered that they were. He asked, "Is the boy still watching them?"

"He's asleep. What town do you come from?" the newcomer asked.

"Jerusalem," the thick-bearded man said. There was a hint of wariness and weariness in his eyes.

The other man at the table answered, "Arimathaea."

The newcomer said, "Jerusalem! Me, too. Near Jerusalem."

"Will you join us?" the Arimathaean asked. His voice was gentler than his friend's. He seemed less wary, less weary.

"Thank you." The newcomer pulled a four-legged stool to the table and sat with his back to the front door.

"We were remembering former times," the soft-spoken Arimathaean said. "We were remembering Jesus of Nazareth, who was crucified."

The newcomer straightened his back and peered first at the Arimathaean's face, and then into the face of the Arimathaean's thick-bearded friend. "I met him once."

"Ah! Good," the Arimathaean said. "Did you witness his dagger-sharp mind? Clever men would plan together how to corner him in a debate, but he was indomitable. But in death –" His eyes rested on his friend. His friend peered back at him quietly and somberly and waited for the Arimathaean to finish his thought. "In death, he was vulnerable and tormented. His words –"

"I didn't see him crucified," the newcomer interrupted.

"Ah."

"I heard rumors that he rose from the dead."

"That's true," the Arimathean said. He gestured toward the thick-bearded man. "My friend and I – "

The bald man interrupted again. "When I heard that he came out of his tomb, I was amazed. I looked for proof. But I learned later that he was making himself known to his disciples here in Galilee while I was searching for him in Jerusalem."

The thick-bearded man said, "Yes, in –"

"Then I heard that the Spirit of the Lord had come on his disciples when they were gathered in Jerusalem. But when that happened, I had left Jerusalem to look for him in Galilee."

The two friends took this in. Then thick-bearded man said, "When I met him for the first time, at night, he spoke of the need to be *reborn* by the Spirit. I didn't know what he was saying.

"Then in Jerusalem, at the time you're talking about, those words became visible. But before that happened in Jerusalem to his disciples, it happened on the Jordan River. He was with John the Baptist –"

"I met him, too."

The thick-bearded man raised his eyebrows at the interruption. He said, "Yes, you said that."

The Arimathaean looked at the thick-bearded man and made a slight gesture with his index finger. The Arimathean man smiled at the newcomer. "Tell us about meeting him."

"Oh. I'm sure that I didn't know him as well as the two of you did."

The thick-bearded man solemnly prodded him. "We'd like to hear about your meeting with Jesus."

The innkeeper brought bread and wine, set it on the table, and left. The two friends offered to share it with the newcomer.

The newcomer ate a glad chunk of bread and drank a thirsty half-cup of wine. Then he gathered his thoughts and said, "I was a young lawyer then. I had good training. I worked hard. But so many people started after me and ended up in front of me."

The innkeeper came back to the room and stood in a corner to listen.

"My would-be father-in-law was wealthy. He hired me for court. But then I lost a long chain of cases.

"He liked me. He tried to be kind. He shook his head and said that I was a parable.

"He said that I sowed much, but reaped little. He said that I put my earnings into a purse with holes. Not to make a picture of my purse, but he was right. He said he could not give his daughter to a man so unknown to blessing.

"I took what he said to heart. So I added righteous stone to righteous stone to build up my religious ways. And I thought that I did well. But nothing changed. I still chased the wind."

He bent his neck and looked briefly down at the table. The thick-bearded man glanced at the lawyer's scalp and then glanced across the table at his friend.

"I had a friend. His father was Egyptian, and his mother was Hebrew. She was of the tribe of Dan. He was a lawyer, like me. He was very clever, but his going was hard, like mine. We were brothers in struggle.

"One day doomed his future. I was not there.

"He represented an Egyptian trader in court. The case went badly for his client. He took his client outside and explained to him what had just happened.

"The client was furious. He cursed my friend, he cursed the judges, he cursed Jerusalem, and he cursed the Almighty." The bald lawyer was silent for a moment, looking between the two friends.

"They spoke in the language of Egypt, of course. But a Hebrew who spoke Egyptian overheard. Our countryman called out to others what he had heard. My friend and his client fled a furious crowd. His client was never seen again.

"My friend was brought to trial before the Sanhedrin. His accuser was still in a righteous rage. Maybe he testified truthfully. Maybe his righteousness and his rage tainted his memory. His testimony was damning against my friend.

"But only one witness testified against my friend. He was the only witness who overheard the conversation and spoke Egyptian. With only one witness, my friend should have been freed.

"But based on the damning testimony of that witness, the judges demanded that my friend say what had happened. He said that his client had blasphemed, but that he had not.

"The judges conferred for over an hour. Then they pronounced him guilty. He took their verdict stoically.

"I was there when the judges pronounced judgment. The judges asked if anyone would speak up for the prisoner before sentencing.

"I should have. He was a good man. But I knew how narrowly I survived from day to day in my profession. It was too risky to stand up for a half-Egyptian blasphemer.

"They sentenced him to ten lashes with a whip. Sentence was carried out immediately.

"Some people said that the judges had compromised among themselves. They found him guilty when they should not have, but then they sentenced him leniently.

"By chance, I met him ten days later. He was about to leave Jerusalem forever through Sheep Gate. I was coming in. I greeted him.

"He shouted at me, 'You could have spoken for me, but you didn't!'

"Without meaning to, I backed away from him. But he closed the gap between us. He shouted, 'You try to be righteous, but you can't be! You paint on righteousness that drips off in rain!'

"When he started shouting, Sheep Gate became blocked because people crowded around to hear.

"He had more to say. 'What you count for righteousness only shuts your heart! You pass sentence on people who aren't like you – people who don't gaze at a warped mirror and primp their fake righteousness!

"And your heart is shut against heaven, because heaven doesn't drench you with blessings! So your righteousness rips you away from everyone else and from heaven itself!

"'Do you know *righteousness*? Your righteousness – it is leprosy!'

"He looked like he wanted to weep. He said, 'Study Moses, my friend. When you do, two laws will stand out. Without them, the others are tombs for proud men.'

"He pushed by me and walked out through Sheep Gate with his head down. The crowd opened for him to pass through.

"His words twisted my gut. Then I searched through the Law of Moses, and two laws stood out. He was right.

"Some time after my friend left Jerusalem forever, I went to the grounds of the Jerusalem Temple. There, Pharisees and Sadducees debated with this Jesus of Nazareth. Their questions were very clever, but they stopped asking him questions because Jesus was crushing them with his answers and awing the crowd.

"When they gave up, I stepped forward. In a way, I was presenting myself to Jesus like a leper might show himself to a priest, to see if his leprosy was gone.

"I said, 'Master, you have spoken well.' Then I asked Jesus, 'What commandments are ahead of all others?'

"He looked at me, and I felt his kindness. He asked me what Moses said.

"I said, 'You must love the Lord with all your heart, soul, and strength; and you must love your neighbor as yourself.'

"Jesus said that I had answered rightly. Not only Jesus but the crowd was pleased with my answer."

The bald lawyer had been looking from the thick-bearded man to the Arimathaean, and sometimes over at the innkeeper. He paused and glanced down at the table again.

Then he looked up. "I still felt shame for failing to help my friend. So I asked, 'But who is my neighbor?'

"Jesus told the story of a man traveling the dangerous road from Jerusalem, where the Temple is, down to Jericho, where King Herod's winter palace is. Bandits fell on this man. They beat and robbed him, and they left him helpless by the side of the road.

"A priest came by, and a Levite came by. They crossed the road to avoid the helpless man. Why not? Bandits leave injured victims as bait and hide themselves nearby to catch other victims.

"But a Samaritan had pity on the helpless man. The Samaritan took him to an inn, and he paid the innkeeper to take care of him. He gave the innkeeper two denarii right away, and he promised to pay any further amount that was needed."

The innkeeper murmured approval.

"Jesus asked me who that man's neighbor was.

"It was pretty obvious who *wasn't* the man's neighbor; so the answer of who *was* his neighbor was obvious, too.

"I think of that story often. I have no right to judge the priest or the Levite. They didn't risk themselves for a stranger. But I didn't risk myself for a friend.

"Here's what I think of most often when I think about that story. You know something about the character of the priest. You know something about the character of the Levite. And you know something about the character of the Samaritan.

"But you don't know anything about the man who was beaten and left helpless by the bandits. You don't know if he was kind or cruel.

"And the Samaritan didn't know, either. But the Samaritan helped him. And they weren't related by blood, friends, religion, or homeland.

"I didn't know Jesus of Nazareth, but he was kind to me. He let me give the answer to my own question in front of a crowd. And he was kind to school me about my own answer. And about myself.

"He perplexes me."

The Arimathaean looked at the bearded man and raised his eyebrows barely more than a hair's breadth. The bearded man made a very slight nod of his head. The

Arimathaean asked, "Where will you go in the morning, friend?"

"Back to Jerusalem. I came to Galilee to make money, but nothing came of it."

The Arimathaean said, "Why don't you come with us? We're going to a wedding in Cana."

The lawyer looked at the Arimathaean. "But I don't know the bridegroom."

The thick-bearded man said, "It doesn't matter. You'll be with us."

The lawyer said to the thick-bearded man, "But I don't have wedding clothes."

The Arimathaean answered, "Like my friend said, you'll be with us."

In their company, the lawyer was happy.

They tolerated him passably well.

10

TURMOIL

JOHN 5:1-15

The young general spoke no Aramaic, so the old man spoke Greek. "I liked numbers," the old man said. "My younger brother didn't. He loved God."

The general was seated. He had curly, short black hair, a cleft chin, and a muscular neck. He was richly dressed in a fine, white military tunic. His purple cape was fastened on his right shoulder by a gold brooch.

The generals he commanded stood in a loose cluster next to and behind him. All had more than their commander's thirty-one years. So had many of the other officers who were gathered around the generals in the open air of the Roman camp. A single Hebrew stood among them, behind the commanding general. He was younger than the commander.

The old man stood with only a simple linen waist-cloth. Hunger had shrunk his face and made his nose seem strangely large. His eyes were sunken. His long white hair and beard flowed like water over stones through a narrow river-channel.

He said, "I was in my nineteenth year. The Temple construction was in its sabbatical year. Work did not stop.

"My father was well-connected. He had gotten me a job helping the architects. That suited me. I had high ambitions in that direction."

A Roman officer asked a question.

"No, the Temple itself was finished," the old man said, responding to the question. He spread his left hand to gesture behind his left shoulder, toward Jerusalem. Jerusalem was visible below them, southeast of the camp, though smoke hid parts of it. The old man's gesture caused the chain that drooped between his wrist-shackles to rattle.

The commanding general apologized for the restraints with a mild shrug. The old man acknowledged the general's apology with a respectful nod. Then he continued to speak of the Temple.

"We Jews did not trust that outsider, that Idumean, King Herod, who built the Temple. This was true even though he converted to our religion and married the daughter of a high priest. But he promised to build the Temple itself within two years. And before he started building, he gathered all of the material needed to do that.

"So we let him tear down the old temple that had stood, such as it was, for five-hundred years. It was built after we had come back from our captivity in Babylon. King Herod did what he said he would. The new temple rose quickly.

"So no, I didn't help with the Temple itself, only with vast grounds and buildings of its campus. These were finished only six years ago, the work of four generations, Your Excellency."

The Roman commander nodded.

The wind had shifted so that it passed over Jerusalem before it passed over the camp. Ash fell.

"My brother, as I said, was godly. He prayed lengthy prayers on his knees. He studied scripture into the night. He would not look on a woman, lest his mind turned to the lesser glory of this sullied world.

"But I was comfortable in the flesh. He encouraged me to pray, for the sake of my soul. But I said that when I prayed my knees hurt badly after not too long, and then it was hard to walk to a brothel."

The Romans snickered.

"I knew of one woman who troubled him. She was the wife of a high official, a counselor to the king. Her name was Judith, after a beautiful and godly woman of our literature. And this Judith was beautiful, like the one she was named for.

"As my brother described it, she might find him by himself and gaze into his eyes, as if she loved his soul. She stirred him. I'm sure he misunderstood; he was only a challenge to her. Or maybe he was an affront to her, because he resisted her power of attraction. Maybe it was a contest to her: her beauty against his godliness.

"But I begrudged him her attention. I thought it should go to one more at ease in the flesh, like me.

"I taunted him. I told him that the kindness of a godly man like him could make her soul shine like her scented hair. It was a running taunt. At first he would ignore me; then he argued against me; then he agreed, but he listed reasons why nevertheless he could not spend time with her.

"And it was doubtful that any man could make her soul shine. She was an appetite, not a soul. Maybe what she did to my family, in which I had fault, pigments my judgment."

An officer standing next to the young general asked a question. Many of the Romans laughed.

With a raised hand, the commander made silence.

"No." The old man spread his hands again. "I don't know a Judith in Jerusalem now." He caught the eye of the Hebrew behind the general, who looked away. "Hunger has reduced us.

"I often passed by the Jerusalem estate of Judith's husband. Sometimes I would see her. She would carry a napkin of Egyptian linen that she held to her upper lip to breathe its perfume. Her husband's family's name was embroidered into it. My father and my brother and I, too, might carry a napkin with our family name, to wipe sweat from our faces with.

"One day, Judith came out of the front gate of her husband's estate. I was passing by, and we were alone. She stood still, dropped her napkin at her feet, and looked away. I bowed down and plucked it from the ground. On one knee, I handed it up to her. She brushed my palm as she took it. Then she walked on.

"Hers was an impulsive, self-centered gesture. No doubt she forgot it before she got to her destination. But afterward, I went past her husband's estate compulsively.

"Until one day I did more. The gate was open, and I knew that her husband was far away. He had gone to Caesarea Maritima, which had just been completed. It was a jewel among Herod's building projects, and Judith's husband had business there.

"My judgment was spectacularly poor. It was the product of my appetite. I had no plan, only urgent hope. I snuck into the garden. Inside, I prowled until I heard laughter on the other side of a hedge. I knew her voice, so I knew it was her.

"I wanted to see what she was doing. There was a narrow gap between two hedges, but there was also a row of closely-planted roses between the gap and me. I pulled out my napkin so I could push the rose stems aside without being pricked.

"But my hand slipped, and the thorns drew blood. Jumping back quickly, I lost my balance and fell onto a bush behind me.

"A man's voice, one I did not know, called out, 'Who's there!?' I ran out of the garden.

"Nobody saw me as I escaped into the street. At my father's house I sat down, perspiring. I leaned my back against the wall and reached for my napkin to wipe my face, the one embroidered with my family's name. Then I realized that I had dropped it in the garden when the roses pricked me and I fell backward.

"I paced, cursed, and beat my thighs with my fists. Having slight character, my reputation was my all-in-all.

"Finally, I got down on my knees. For the first time in my life, I prayed at length. I promised God that if he would deliver me from this humiliation, I would serve him faithfully all my days. I would worship him constantly, I would never look at a woman with lust, and I would care for the destitute. And so on.

"Our porter interrupted my prayers. He said that officials demanded to see me. They flooded in behind the porter.

"I stood. I had prayed, but I knew that heaven has a stone ear to a man like me. God did not have his hand on me; instead, fleshy gratifications had a hook through my nose.

"The chief officer demanded to know where my brother was.

"It took a few seconds to grasp the literal meaning of his words. It took a few more seconds to grasp what his words implied. It took a few seconds after that to make my answer.

"I said that at this time of day he would be at the Temple.

"The officer said my brother would not be the first scoundrel to hope for refuge there. They left.

"I had to sit in order not to fall. I pressed my head to my knees, until I was no longer light-headed.

"It was too clear: I had surprised Judith with a lover. When they found my napkin, they had made a preemptive accusation. They had erred about who had invaded the garden, maybe because Judith thought more on my brother than on me.

"And because of the napkin, if they discovered that my brother was innocent, they would know that I was at fault. We looked enough alike that sometimes people confused one of us for the other.

"To myself, I justified my failure to come to my brother's defense with the officials. I considered that my brother was better able to bear any penalty than I was. His life was good; certainly heaven would take up his cause.

"I heard hurried steps. My brother rushed into the room and stood front of me. He was sweating, as I had been, and his hands trembled.

"'Brother,' he said, 'people say that I tried to lie with the Counselor's wife. It's not true, but they are hunting me. Brother, why are you smiling?'

"I answered, 'Because, Brother, nobody will believe that about you.'

"'But, Brother, people will remember that I was not in the Temple today. It's true. I was – I was elsewhere.' He scanned the room as if searching for hidden ears.

"He looked down. He blushed. 'I was with a woman. A low woman.'

"I was astonished. But I said, 'Still, Brother, your reputation is good. Deny the lies. People will remember that you have always been truthful.'

"'But what if they ask where I was? What will I say?'

"I considered this. Before I answered, he said, 'Brother.'

"'Yes?'

"'Brother, will you say that I was here, with you?'

"I was astonished again. Then I looked in his face. I said, 'You are my brother'. He embraced me.

"We sent a messenger to the officials at the forum, where court was held. I told him to say that my brother and I were on our way to answer the false charges against him.

"When we got to the forum, my father stood among the onlookers. His face was the color of flecks of ash. We waited for more than an hour as they assembled twenty-three judges. That number showed the seriousness of the charges.

"I stood by my father and whispered that everything would be fine. I said that over and over. I sounded angry, even to myself.

"The judges assembled. They sat on their raised platform. Judith came in and stood in front of the judges, but to one side.

"When my brother went forward, Judith cried out. She held one hand over her stomach. She bent forward and seemed to weep. She covered her mouth with her other hand. Several men walked up and surrounded her. Their eyes translated my brother into a demon. He returned their looks with wide-eyed dread.

"The chief judge called for the witnesses. Being a woman, Judith could not testify.

"The first witness was the handsome son of a wealthy grain merchant. He was in his early twenties. He said that he had passed by Judith's home and heard her cry out, and he had charged into her garden. There he interrupted my brother, who had seized her by her hair and was trying to tear off her clothing.

"His servant said likewise.

"Judith swooned when the servant finished his testimony. Men helped her to stand. She turned to the judges and tearfully asked, 'What is my sin that this has happened to me?' The chief judge sat stern-faced. Several assistant judges glanced over at my brother.

"The chief judge demanded my brother's explanation.

"When my brother spoke, his words ran together. The chief judge had to stop him twice and tell him to start over. He constantly licked his lips. He often stopped to swallow. His hands shook.

"He said that he had not done the thing that he had been accused of. He said that he was not in this woman's garden at all. He said that he was home at the time of the event with me, his brother. He said that I had come to court to say that.

"A prosecutor had my blood-specked napkin. He marched up to my brother and held the stitching with our family name in front of my brother's face. He said, 'Tell the judges, then, how your napkin got into this young woman's garden!' My brother stared at it and shook his head faintly. The prosecutor turned and looked up at the judges. He too shook his head.

"The chief judge called me forward. He told me to say what I knew. I looked down at my feet. I said, 'My brother has always been known as a truthful person.' My face was red. My shame was real.

"The judge asked me, 'Was your brother with you when the witnesses say he came to her?'

"I continued to look down. I said, again, 'My brother has always been known as a truthful person.'

"The chief judge demanded, 'Tell us: *Was he with you?!*'

"I repeated what I had said before.

"The chief judge ordered my brother to jail. He said that the court would give its verdict that evening.

"They chained my brother's wrists. Four officials, one on each side of him, led him out. There was no blood in his face. At the doorway, he looked over his shoulder in my direction, but I don't know if he saw me.

"My father turned to me with tears. He put his arms around me. He said that he understood what I had to do, and that I could not lie. He was glad that I had not, because then he might have had two sons under judgment.

"When we got home, father wanted me to stay with him for company, but I went to be alone. I did in fact feel under judgment.

"Everyone wants a long life. But suddenly I wished for a particularly long one. I hoped to outlive my sinfulness before I came to heaven's throne for judgment.

"I dropped to my knees next to my bed. I prayed for heaven to give me the will to stand up for my brother and to say the truth. As I prayed that, I felt a peace come over me.

"But I rejected the peace. I argued turbulently that my brother had trapped himself by lying and was responsible for his own doom.

"The peace was gone. But still I had a sense of presence, of an outside attentiveness. It provoked me to regret my resistance to the peace. I continued to resist, but more weakly. The presence left.

"Its absence made me uneasy. I wondered if this was what a messenger from God felt like. So I called after it, 'If that's what you want, Lord, I will do it.'

"But I was determined to wait to see what the judges decided. I hoped that I would not have to condemn myself in the court of men. I feared them more than God, because their judgment was swift.

"My father and I stood with the onlookers in court in the evening. The judges came in and sat. My father clasped my arm above my elbow for support. His grip hurt my arm.

"Then an official came into the courtroom. An assistant judge asked him why the prisoner was not with him.

"He told the judges that the prisoner had hanged himself.

"There was silence. Then a man next to the official said that at least the prisoner had died quickly. The official said that the prisoner did not fall far enough to break his neck. He had strangled.

"A man next to me whispered to a neighbor, 'The kicking death.'

"Court adjourned. One of the judges walked up to my father and put his hand on my father's shoulder. This was a generous gesture.

"Then the judge turned to me. He put his hand flat on my chest and called me a good man. He urged me not to feel responsible for my brother's suicide. He said that everyone could see that I had tried to protect him. But, he said, the judges were skilled. They had been careful to note the difference between what I seemed to say and what I really said. He told me to have courage.

"Then he turned back to my father. He told my father that the offices who went to our house had found me in prayer.

"Every day after the trial, my father thought of my brother. He would murmur from the psalm: 'If I climb to heaven, you are there; if I make my bed in hell, behold, you are there.' He died within half a year.

"I lost use of my legs soon after my father died."

The commander held his hand up to the prisoner, and the prisoner stopped speaking. Then the commander looked behind him and raised a finger to an officer. The officer came forward and bent down to the commander. The commander whispered to him, and the officer left. The commander gestured for the prisoner to continue.

"I was watching the transfer of a great stone from the quarry to the temple grounds. The quarry was above the temple. Great stones were quarried round and rolled to the building site. There, they were cut into usable blocks. The workers were using ropes to slow the roll of the stone. All of the ropes broke at once, and the stone got away from the workers.

"I was looking in the wrong direction. The man next to me jumped out of the way. The workers shouted, but I was somehow oblivious.

"The stone collided with me and a wall almost simultaneously. It threw me. It might have killed me, or it might have left me unharmed.

"Instead, I woke weak and in pain. Soon, everything below my waist was numb."

A Roman officer asked the old man whether he really felt nothing. The officer made an obscene gesture with his finger below his waist. Others laughed. The commanding general smirked.

The old man admitted, "It was as you say.

"My brother and my father were gone, and my kin shunned me. People interpreted the crippling event as divine judgment. The ropes knew.

"My wealth dissipated. I poured out most of it right away. Most of it went to the Temple and to alms; I tried to buy forgiveness. Some of it went to doctors.

"I stayed at a pool beneath the north side of the Temple. The blind, the lame, and the paralyzed abided there. As I lay by the water, stone by stone, a wall went up between the Temple and me.

"Being lame, I could not go into the Temple. But I could hear hammers and the grinding sound of stones being fitted into place. I could hear workers cheer as one part or another part of the campus was completed.

"The pool where I spent my time was really two pools. It had five porticos that gave shade. One portico was on each of the four sides of the pools, and one was set on pillars that rose up from the wall between the two pools.

"One pool was always being re-filled by a slow stream of water. The other had still water. The still water had to be replenished from the living water of the other pool. Only then was it useful for cleansing and healing.

"When water was released from one pool to the other, it would stir the pool getting the water. At the moment when the living water entered it, the otherwise still pool had its greatest ritual purity, its greatest healing power.

"I heard about, but I did not see, the three-thousand zealots who rebelled against King Herod. I heard about, but I did not see, their slaughter on the grounds of the Temple. I heard them cry out. And I heard people weep for them after they were dead.

"I heard about, but I did not see, the great eagle, the symbol of Rome, that King Herod put over the door of the Temple. I heard about, but I did not see, the brave men who tore the eagle down. I did not see them roasted alive, but I smelled their burning flesh.

"I yearned to be among them, even to die with them, rather than live uselessly waiting for the waters to stir.

"I had given up hope. I grieved my sins, and I grieved my poor brother and my poor father. I prayed for them. I drank my own tears.

"And after thirty-eight years, it seemed like I had grown old in a day.

"I had changed. A rich young man with a promising future has a different spirit than a hopeless object of revulsion."

Stewards passed among the Romans bearing trays with gold and silver cups of wine.

"You would think that after thirty-eight years, when I regained my legs, that would occur with tumult. I had thought that if such a miracle were to happen, it might happen dramatically, like Ezekiel's vision."

A general asked who Ezekiel was.

"Ezekiel was a prophet. God gave him a vision of a valley of dry bones. He heard a great rattling noise. He saw scattered bones assemble themselves into skeletons. Sinews and flesh covered the skeletons, and the former skeletons stood up as men. The Hebrew among you can tell you more about that.

"But it wasn't that way with me. If anything, my cure was a placid event.

"A stranger came to me at the pool. Among all of the blind and lame and paralyzed there, he asked me if I wanted to be well. I explained that I was unable to do anything; when the water was stirred, I could not enter it. Nobody would help me, and others went in ahead.

"That's how I saw my plight. High walls shut me out of heaven. And I was helpless to seize the scarce help that heaven gave.

"Then the man said to stand up, take up my mat, and walk. That's all he said. I stood up. In awe, I looked at my legs and feet, and I and walked around. My legs and feet were strong. I looked for the man who told me to stand up, but he was gone. But people in the crowd saw me walking, and they were amazed.

"I have been fully restored ever since."

A sallow officer at the edge of the Roman crowd asked if the old man had been restored in every way. The Romans around him glanced at each other and snorted. The old man said that, Yes, he was.

"People shouted that I should go to the Temple to give glory to God. I myself was eager to do that.

"In the Temple, I expected people to join me in giving glory to God when they learned that I could walk again after thirty-eight years. They did not. They complained that I was violating the Sabbath by carrying my mat.

"But I could not help myself. The man who had made me walk again after almost four decades told me to take up my palate and walk. For him, I would have thrown myself off a high temple wall.

"That man found me in the Temple. When he found me, I worshiped him. He told me not to sin anymore, so that nothing worse would happen to me.

"When people ask me if I have managed not to sin, the simple answer is No. I shuffle off one layer of sin, but always another layer lies beneath it.

"But I have loved the man who forgave my sins. I have loved my God. I have done what I could do to serve his people.

"When my spirit is too weak to control my flesh, I remember my thirty-eight lost years. I remember what he said, not to sin lest something worse should happen to me. I think about what might be worse than those thirty-eight years. That reminds me to fear God, and that fear beats down my flesh.

"It is well that I suffered for so long. I have tried to live up to the oath I made to God as a panicked young man. I strive to make my Lord glad that he showed mercy to me. Without the passage of time, I would have quickly forgotten that oath. Then, maybe I would have found out what is worse than thirty-eight lost years.

"To serve heaven and human-kind, I have gone without food, without shelter, without safety, without warmth, without honor. Sometimes not. I do not reject a feast when it is offered, nor refuse wine when I have it."

Several Romans nudged each other and grinned. The commander looked behind him, made an election, and waved an officer forward. The officer and a steward met in front of the old man. The officer gave the old man his silver cup, and the steward replenished it with wine.

The old man nodded to the general. Then he held the cup to his eyes. He squinted at it as he rotated it with both hands. He asked, "Is this from the Temple?"

An officer said that it was.

The old man bowed his head again to the young commander. Then he kneeled on the ground and put the cup, filled with wine, in front of him.

He stood again. "The Lord God Almighty made me part of his kingdom. If I can do without luxuries, that is the grace of my Lord Jesus, crucified under Pontius Pilate. The tomb could not contain him."

The Romans laughed. The old man heard them without expression or resentment.

"It is he who made me walk again. He did that with only a few words of command."

The Romans quieted.

"I was not in the Temple when your prefect took money from the Temple's treasury. Many of our people counseled looking away from this offense. Others were impatient to throw off Rome. Blood prevailed.

"We slaughtered your garrison. Then we defeated the legion you sent."

Grave-side silence prevailed among the Romans.

"I returned to Jerusalem. I came to share the suffering that I knew would come.

"Your four legions surrounded us. You broke through our walls. But the proverb is right: one who breaks down a wall is stung by a serpent. You paid a high price in men.

"You took one piece of the city, then another. You pressed your faces forward, breathing death in our faces. We could not fly to the wilderness, because you contained us.

"I ministered in Jerusalem during the siege and the fighting. While I had strength, I tended the wounded. I scrounged food for the young and the vulnerable. Then there was none to scrounge.

"When I had no strength, I offered prayers.

"In the end, many pious Hebrew men threw themselves from high walls. They had cried to heaven for help, but heaven seemed not to hear. They had cried *violence*, but God did not save. They hoped that their sacrifice would make heaven pity Jerusalem. Maybe heaven does.

"But here you sit, Your Excellency. We tore down your eagle; the eagle returns to eat our flesh. Its god is its might."

The Romans hurrahed.

The old man eyed them wearily. "You have slaughtered us. You have killed our men, our women, and our children."

There was another hurrah.

"You stacked great piles of wood around the Temple. You lit the fire. The fire burst the stones. The great temple that the Roman King Herod made with genius fell by the Roman genius for havoc."

Another hurrah.

An officer shouted from the back.

The old man repeated the question. "Where is our God now?' The old man looked to the sky for a moment. "In times past, God sometimes kept us away from the furnace. Sometimes, he put us by the furnace. We felt its fire on our faces, but he kept us out of it. Sometimes he has met us in the flames. Again, the Hebrew among you can explain this.

"My years have been few compared to my ancestors, but I am counted ancient.

"Heaven took a lifetime from me. Then the Almighty gave me back a lifetime to replace the one he took, and he added to it.

"I still have not outlived my sinfulness. But now I know the vastness of the mercy of the Lord, which is like the vastness of the heavens. It is greater than my sins. It is greater than my father's sins, my mother's sins, and my brother's sins. I hope to see them again.

> The fig tree does not bloom;
> > The grape vine has no fruit.
> The olive tree is naked;
> > The field gives no grain.
> The fold holds no flock;
> > The stall has no herd.
> But the Lord is my delight;
> > God is my salvation and my joy.
> He is my strength;
> > He makes my feet like deer's feet on high.

"In victory, do not sin, Excellency. Make peace with Jesus Christ and with his Father. His Father showed our prophet Moses a bush that burned but was not consumed. Jesus has been given the keys to death and hell.

"Herod, who built our temple, was king because your general Pompey conquered our nation. Our forebears pleaded with Pompey not to violate the temple's holiest place. The more they pleaded, the more sure he was that vast treasure waited for him in the innermost part of the Temple.

"So Pompey went in despite our pleas not to do so. He found an empty chamber.

"The emptiness he stood in was sacred far above his knowing. Like a certain empty tomb would later be.

"After that, he was sifted like wheat. He died in Egypt. Some say that his downfall was hubris. But his downfall was greed and ignorance."

There were hostile murmurs from the Romans. The young commander eyed the old man coldly. The old man met the general's eye, looked to the sky, and closed his own eyes for part of minute. Ashes flecked his face.

The commander beckoned to an officer. The officer came forward, and the general whispered to him.

The old man opened his eyes and said, "Be wise. The palaces of the compassionate will rise over the ruins of the cruel."

The Hebrew behind the general moved to the back of the crowd.

"I was crippled for thirty-eight years. After that, thirty-eight years passed, and the Temple and its grounds were completed.

"King Herod began to build the Temple. Forty-five years passed, and Jesus the Messiah began his ministry. From then to now is forty-five years.

"The Temple itself was completed before the rest of the temple grounds. Forty-four years after that, I was healed. Jesus ministered in that time. From then to now is forty-four years.

The officer who had whispered with the young commander stepped forward to the old man. He kicked the silver cup away, and the wine entered the earth. He expertly grasped old man's beard, and he forced the old man down on his hands and knees.

The old man looked beyond the Romans and whispered, "In the name of Jesus the Christ, I can bear your sting."

The commanding general succeeded his father as emperor of the Roman Empire. He died two years after that, while he was still young.

11

FORTUNE

Matt 19:16-22; Mark 10:17-22; Luke 18:18-22

The sea came to the bottom of his naked chest. Water dripped from his long grey hair and beard. He looked at the man standing on the shore, some seventy feet away. Then, with both hands, he lifted a fat fish out of the water and over his head. He tilted his head back and laughed. The man on the shore laughed, too.

He frog-kicked toward the shore, with his head bobbing and the fish over his head. When he could walk easily, he stood and waded in. He plopped the fish down next to the fire. There were two other fish already.

"Enough?" He laughed again.

"Enough!" the other man agreed. He also laughed.

They cooked the fish. They ate.

"I spoke to a woman today", Jude said. Jude was the man who had come out of the water. He grinned. "She didn't like my rags. She was grinding wheat into flour. I asked her why she did that all day long."

"What did she say?"

"She said that if she didn't need bread, she wouldn't grind."

"What else did she say?"

"I asked her if she was grinding for her husband. She said she grinds for whoever pays her."

The other man laughed. "Her husband must be both pleased and not pleased."

Jude laughed, too.

The fire crackled.

The other man breathed deeply and smiled. "Jude."

"Yes."

"Tell me your story."

"What? Again?"

"Please."

They sat and watched the sun dip into the sea.

"I was rich. I had houses and fields and servants and trading-businesses. These were in Jerusalem and Lydda. It was my inheritance from my parents. God rest their souls."

"Amen."

"I had a brother. He had bread-and-lentils money, but not more. He had wasted his inheritance.

"He lived off me. His tastes were rich. He resented me, because I had held onto my wealth."

"So there was contention?"

"There was. And not just from him. There were lawsuits. Some of them were from business my brother did for me. People sued me because of him. And sometimes people sued me – just because.

"A surprising number of the lawsuits went badly. They were vexatious, particularly when I was told I would win, and I *believed* that I was right, but I lost.

"I was occupied holding onto my fortune from lawsuits, from tax collectors, from kin who needed help. Sometimes the kin wanted extravagant help.

"My escape from the daily pressure was the study of sacred scrolls.

"I tithed. I contributed to the education of children in impoverished, pious families. I brought sacrifices to the Temple for atonement. I honored the Sabbath. I was scrupulous in ritual, faithful to the Commandments. I poured myself into knowing how to live a godly life. Whatever my offense was, I wanted to remove it, so that I might enjoy my wealth with contentment.

"But I had no contentment. The lawsuits angered me.

"And my brother angered me. He would deal sharply with a merchant, and that would harm my name. He would bully my servants, and I hated that. He spent money in brothels."

The other man asked, "There was no good in him?"

"There was. He lent freely from what he had. He made friends.

"As to his disagreeable practices, I tried to stop him. But I was a big dog intimidated by a little dog.

"As time went by, instead of confronting him, I would scold his shadow when I was alone.

"And the judges who ruled against me – I would scold their shadows, too. I would scold the shadows of greedy tax collectors. All day long, I had furious conversations with the shadows of people who were somewhere else being happy while I boiled.

"I asked God what my sin was, that I had no contentment. I asked him to show me what to do, and I would do what it took.

"I hired a famous lawyer at great cost. He was a sharp-elbowed negotiator and a courtroom viper. He was handsome, and his eyes gleamed with shrewdness. I had confidence in him.

"Shortly after he took on my cases, he sat down with me at my home. My brother sat with us. The lawyer smilingly laid out his plans for turning around my legal fortunes.

"At the end of our meeting, he talked about an offer from the other side in a particular case. The other side wanted to bring the case to a close on terms that I could live with. I was glad, because that case pricked my conscience.

"My lawyer grinned. 'Your opponent hired the worst lawyer he could find. His lawyer is famous for losing cases. That's why his head is hairless like a citron.' He laughed. 'Reject the offer. We'll win.'

"As he said this, I remembered the psalm that goes:

> The unity of brothers is so good!
> > It is like oil on the head,
> That runs down on the beard,
> > On Aaron's beard that flows to his chest,
> Like the dew on Mount Hermon,
> > That quenches the thirsty earth.
> There the Lord ordained his blessing,
> > Life without end.

"I said, 'Let's agree with the other side. I don't think –'

"My brother interrupted me. 'You'll be ridiculed. But winning this case will frighten away every other grasping lick-penny.'

"The lawyer pointed to my brother. He said, 'Listen to him.' I said nothing.

"A month went by. God seemed to give me no signal about how to gain a peaceful spirit.

"One day, I went to the Temple. On the way, I passed a man in rags. His hair was long – a disgrace. He was so filthy that I was surprised that his bare feet left no stain on the white stones of the street. As I passed him, I move away from his smell. For some reason, he lingered in my memory, like his smell lingered in the air.

"This was the time of the ministry of Jesus. He and his followers were in the Temple that day. The poor of the city surrounded him.

"They had little to give to the Temple's treasury, if anything. I felt lofty in comparison, because I gave gold and silver. Some priests blessed and flattered me.

"I had heard of Jesus. I was curious. I wanted to speak with him, but the poor and the sick were between him and me.

"I stood at the edge of the crowd, expecting Jesus to lift his eyes to a man of standing, which my servants and my clothing showed me to be. He never did.

"He was a man of renown, so his behavior baffled me. He seemed devoted to these people whom God had not seen fit to bless. His closest followers were fishermen, tax collectors, even a man said to have been a bandit.

"Yet he was famous for miracles. Blind men seeing. The lame walking. Demons expelled.

"It was not lost on me that this rootless miracle-worker was profoundly blessed, yet I lacked even the blessing of restful sleep.

"I looked on the down-and-out men around him. I could smell them. And I thought 'Their blood is precious in his sight.' Those words came quietly to my mind, but, once there, they had heft. Later in the day, on the roof patio of my Jerusalem home, I searched for them in scrolls. They came from a psalm of Solomon. The psalm spoke of Solomon's care and concern for the poor.

"I followed my thoughts to another psalm that spoke of the happiness of those who consider the poor, and of how God delivers people in distress – people who consider the poor.

"Then Job rose up in my thoughts. Job had the courage to declare his innocence after heart-killing catastrophes and condemnation by his friends. Job was brave because he was righteous. That was his rock of confidence. And much of the good he did was to care for the poor and the oppressed. I compared Job's courage to my timidity.

"I thought of Leviticus. I thought about Moses's commandment to leave gleanings in the field after harvest, for the poor to collect. I read in Deuteronomy about generosity to those in need.

"And I thought of Jesus and his attention to the poor and the needy. I thought of the mark of favour that God had put on everything about him and everything he did.

"It was like heaven was opening its mind to me. I started to think of ways that I could set aside more of my wealth to help the needy.

"The thought possessed me. If this inspiration was from God, then maybe, I thought, putting it into practice would bless me with peace, rest at bedtime, a clear conscience, favor in law-courts, and courage, which I craved. I wondered if God had withheld peace from my mind to make this bargain with me, to give me this understanding.

"As I sat and thought, my brother stomped up the stairs to the roof. He stood close in front of me, looking down. He said that he had just spoken to Jesus. I was curious, so I asked, 'What did he say?'

"He answered, 'Jesus said that you should divide your inheritance with me.'

"I asked, 'Divide?'

"He pointed to my face: 'Half'. He pointed to his chest: 'Half'.

"My brother's announcement pricked my fear and woke it up. My thoughts of generosity scattered. Money was my fortress against being like the people who surrounded Jesus in the Temple. And Jesus was saying to give away half? That seemed like reckless generosity. The idea made me short of breath.

"Yet my brother could be opportunistic with facts. I stood and walked past him, down to the street. I went to the Temple. I hoped Jesus would be there.

"I dreaded the idea that Jesus had laid on me the burden of giving up half my wealth. If that were so, I wanted to hear it myself from the lips of the man, this prophet who did the miracles.

"I was willing to pay a price for contentment. Certainly I wanted no strife with God. But what Jesus had said seemed too great.

"Two things happened on my way to the Temple. First, I passed the house of a neighbor. His home had a single level and a roof patio. His young son was at the front of the roof, reciting his lessons. I heard him recite a part of a psalm: 'Teach me to do your will; for you are my God; your spirit is good – lead me into the land of uprightness.'

"I slowed. I would have stopped to listen to more, but my urgent need to confront Jesus about my fortune drove me on.

"The second thing was that, before I got to the Temple, Jesus was coming my way in the street. I ran up to him. I knelt in front of him. I intended to ask him if it was true, what my brother had said.

"He stopped, and everyone behind him stopped. He and they looked at me. I looked up at him.

"I was uncomfortable, because so much depended on what he was about to say. I called him *Good Teacher*.

"He asked me why I called him *good*, because no-one was good – only God alone.

"When he spoke of the goodness of God, I remembered the psalm that I had heard on the way there: 'Teach me to do your will; for you are my God; your spirit is good.'"

"And I remembered that God commanded all of the things that I'd been thinking of on my roof – to care for the poor, for the oppressed, for the outsider, for the widow, the orphan, the sick, and the naked – because he was *good*. If his goodness needed proof, that care, that love, was that proof.

"So suddenly I was thinking about bigger things than my inheritance; when I spoke to Jesus again, I asked a bigger question.

"I asked Jesus about salvation. I asked him what I needed do to be saved. I wanted to know what a God that was good and who called for his people to be good – what that God required.

"Jesus said that I needed to follow the Law. He listed several commandments.

"I told Jesus that I had followed those commandments from my youth. And that was true: I had. But those practices, however they blessed others, gave me no peace. I wanted an answer that would give me peace – even if that answer meant giving away half my wealth.

"There was great kindness in Jesus's eyes. He held me with them. Then he said that I lacked one thing. He said that if I wanted to be perfect, I had to sell everything that I owned and give the money to the poor. He said that that would give me treasure in heaven. Then I had to follow him.

"When he said that, I nearly lost my balance and fell into him. I gaped at him. I did not believe that he had said that. I didn't speak. I stood up to get away – I stumbled away, really. As I went, I kept looking back at him. He turned his attention to the people behind him. I only saw his back.

"Before I had gone too far, one of his disciples caught up with me. I didn't like his look. He seemed predatory.

"He said that Jesus expected a gift, and he asked what I had to give him. Somewhat dazed, I gave him what was in my purse. He left without saying anything else.

"Later, as I sat on my roof, I got angry. I started answering the shadow of Jesus like I answered the shadows of my brother, and the judges, and the tax collectors. It makes you feel a little less impotent to do that. You always win when you box against shadows.

"Except that didn't happen this time. I remembered what Jesus said about God's goodness. And I thought that if his spirit were good, then the only right thing was to do his will.

"I lacked Job's confidence because my spirit was misshapen. Jesus had suggested that my spirit was not good, and he was right. The imperfect had met the perfect.

"I thought about God's greatness. I had a fortune that made me known in Jerusalem. But God owned the earth, everything under the earth, and everything over the earth. He was not only good, unlike me; he was vast. I was paltry.

"I couldn't box against God, so I started bargaining. I committed myself to giving away half of my wealth. Or approximately half. Or half of my earnings each year, if not half of my actual fields and other wealth.

"I felt that I had negotiated peace at a high price, but it was a price that I could bear.

"Then my porter brought up to my roof a servant of the famous lawyer I had hired. He gave me news about a lawsuit. He said that we had lost.

"I said, 'But your master said that the other side had the worst possible lawyer.'

"He replied, 'I am given to know that that statement is correct.'

"'Your master said that we would win.'

"'My master sends his regrets. He says that he can seek victory in a more exalted court – more exalted than the one that gave this verdict.' When he mentioned the court that had ruled against me, he made a contemptuous, flicking gesture with the fingers of one hand.

"I hung my head. I waived away the servant. I brooded.

"That night, as I turned in my bed, I again asked God for peace. And I thought of the psalm that said that a king is not saved by an army, and a mighty man is not saved by his strong arm. That made me think of my famous, costly lawyer. And I thought of my riches.

"And I walked up the steps to look at the stars. I was clever enough to know when to send a man to Lydda to buy wheat or to sell linen; God set the constellations. He made the sky, the earth, and every human soul.

"I grew calm; I went to bed and fell asleep. I woke my servants before first light. I told them to get ready to sell everything I owned. And to distribute the money to the poor.

"Some of them told my brother – it was their livelihoods, too. He came to stop me. He couldn't, of course. But he argued that if I wanted to destroy my own security, I could go ahead, but what about him? He grew louder and more desperate.

"As I started to dismantle my fortune, I was anxious for a different reason. I had no confidence that as my fortune shrank, I would continue to give it away. I expected to lose heart and retreat into trusting in my now-reduced riches.

"As my possessions were sold, word spread. The poor came to my door for alms. They mixed with the merchants and the traders and others who came looking for bargains. Everybody left happy.

"The difference was that the poor praised God, and they prayed for me. Their prayers lifted me. I started feeling more peace, more confidence, more hope, and more love. As more was sold, and more was given, I was more blessed by more prayers.

"It was the opposite with my brother. He groaned over every departure of my riches. When he saw that there was nothing he could do, he bellowed out every sin and fault that I had, and some that he invented, and he burst out of my house. On the way out, he roughly bumped some of my servants. Outside, he collided with a beggar who was looking the wrong way. The beggar's new coins sprayed all over the street."

"So he was furious?"

"Yes. And that made me sad. But I had nothing he wanted, nothing to keep from him, and I was beyond his ability to manipulate me. I wasn't angry at him. And when I wasn't angry at him, I loved him.

"At one point, my servants told me that a filthy beggar wanted a robe and a cloak and sandals in addition to the coins they were giving out. I told them to give him a robe and a cloak and sandals.

"They came back, because the beggar had another request. He had told my servants that there was someone who would be greatly blessed by also getting a robe and a cloak and sandals.

"I laughed at the idea of a beggar being munificent with my wealth. I shouted, 'Give it to him!' I felt such joy.

"When almost everything was gone, I gave money to my servants, thanked them, and left wearing only a linen cloth. I looked for Jesus, to tell him that I had done what he had said to do, and to follow him.

"It was night. It was the first day of the Festival of Unleavened Bread. I searched. Finally, I heard a rumour that a crowd of men had gone looking for him on the Mount of Olives, at a place called Gethsemane.

"I left the city. Ahead of me, I saw a cluster of torches in the Kidron Valley headed in the direction of the Mount of Olives.

"I followed the torches up the Mount of Olives. As I got close, I heard shouting. Suddenly, several of the disciples of Jesus ran past me, in a panic. I spun around and watched them run away. I was amazed. I didn't understand.

"Then I heard more running from behind. Men with swords came at me. I fled after the disciples, but one of the men grabbed the linen cloth I wore. I shook it off and outran them all.

"They crucified Jesus. I followed him to Golgotha to see with my eyes what they had done. I saw from a distance. They nailed his heels and hands to a wooden cross. He hung, slowly suffocating, like a criminal. His clothes were in a pile at the base of the cross that he was dying on. Soldiers were picking through them.

"I was in disbelief. This had happened to the man that I had given up my inheritance to follow. I sat and wept. I wanted to melt into the dirt, and never remember anything, and never be remembered by anyone.

"I wept for a long time, until I had no more strength to weep.

"Then I looked at him again. I remembered his love as he looked down at me. I remembered the love and joy I felt as I gave away what I owned, with all of the poor of Jerusalem blessing me with their prayers.

"I remembered the love and attention that he gave to the needy in the Temple. And suddenly, I realized that he had made me feel love like he felt.

"And I realized that if I was naked, he was naked, like me – and he was a great man of God. His nakedness seemed like a precious gift, because it took away my shame at being naked.

"At that moment, I felt someone cover my shoulders with a robe. I touched it, looked at it, and turned to see where it came from. It was the ragged, foul-smelling beggar who I had passed on the way to see Jesus for the first time. But he was washed. And he was wearing my robe and my cloak, and he was laying the other cloak next to me, and a pair of sandals. Then he turned and walked off.

"As I wrapped the clothes around me, I looked again at Jesus. I saw his suffering and his godliness. I began weeping again, but this time for him.

"Good came from what I had done. For instance, a field that I sold was re-sold and became a cemetery for the poor. It became known as the Field of Blood."

The sun was down, the fire was burning low, and the moon was rising. Jude's companion said, "Is it time?"

Jude said, "Yes, it is."

The two men knelt in the sand and prayed. They prayed for God's kingdom. They prayed for the sick and the poor and the hopeless. They prayed for people that they knew and for people that they had never heard of. They prayed for the woman grinding wheat into flour. They prayed for rulers, and for preachers, and for the church. They prayed for the enemies of the church. They prayed for a long time as the moon rose, and they praised God. Then the rested from their prayers.

Jude said, "Tomorrow, you'll tell me your story, right?"
"Again?"
"Please."
"Yes."
They shared a blanket. The other man said, "Jude?"
"Yes?"
"We'll die one day, you know."

"Yes, we will."
"Praise God."
"Praise God."
They slept. As the moon shone on them, their faces were much alike.

12

CALLING

Matt. 20:29-34; Mark 10:46-52; Luke 18:35-43

"After what I saw, I wanted to pluck out my eyes. But I needed them to find my friend, even though I didn't know what he looked like."

People in the market square were buying and selling, counting coins, chatting, sitting. Some were glad, some were glum. Some were wondering what would happen in the next week or month or year.

The man spoke to all who came near. Some listened, some didn't.

"Every day, my friend and I sat under a tree beside the broad, stone-paved road out of Jericho that led to Jerusalem.

"We were aware of the tree. We could feel it, and we could hear wind rustle its leaves.

"And we sensed each other's presence, even when we didn't speak.

"We heard footfalls of people coming and going. Some were quick, some plodded. Some thudded, some were light. Sometimes we heard many, sometimes there were few. Our ears were acute to the sound of a coin dropped onto the rag in front of us.

"We might hear the chirp or flutter of a bird. But when we didn't hear it, the bird didn't exist to us.

"Largely, we sat in a void. Except when it rained. Then the void became a contoured world of things and substances. And thunder put a vault over us, the vault that a sighted person sees every time he looks up at the sky.

"The morning breathed spring on my face. It was shortly before Passover in a year when only one side of the tree above us grew leaves.

"When my friend came and sat, I asked him, 'Where did you sleep?'

"He answered, 'In a ditch.'

"I laughed.

"He asked, 'Why do you laugh?'

"'Because a ditch funnels the wind. Who would sleep in a ditch?'

"He laughed, too. 'You're right. I didn't sleep in a ditch.'

"I asked him: 'Do you know the prayer, "God, make me neither rich nor poor?"'

"'Which one?'

"'God, make me neither rich nor poor. Because if I am rich, I will forget that I need you. But if I am poor, I will embarrass you by stealing.'"

"'Yes, I think I do.'

"'What do you think of that prayer?'

"He said, 'I think that we are poor, but we can't steal, because we are blind.'

"I laughed again. 'Exactly.'

"He said, 'What would you do if you could see?'

"We had talked about this before. I turned the question back to him: 'What would you do?'

"'I don't know. A beggar who can work gets little kindness. I'd become a laborer, I suppose.'

"I said, 'I'd just go. Walk. Everywhere. And I'd look at everything.'

"My friend said, 'Your father used to take you to Jerusalem.'

"'If he were alive and I could see, now I'd be taking him.'

"We sat quietly for a time. Someone dropped a coin in front of us.

"I said, 'Peace on you and your house!' I told my friend, 'I had a bad dream last night.'

"'I had a good one.'

"'What was yours?'

"He said, 'I was in a pleasant wood. It was cool. There were birds, a soft wind in the treetops, bees, sweet smells, and a stream. And people brought me whatever I wanted.'

"I replied, 'I was nowhere, alone. I walked and walked, and there was no sound, no wind, nobody. I called out, and there wasn't any answer.'

"Another person dropped a coin. She said, 'Jesus is coming this way.'

"I said, 'Thank you for saying! Blessings on you and your house!' I don't know what my friend's reaction was. He didn't reply vocally.

"I tried to remember everything that I had heard about Jesus. I had a good memory for things I heard, because I craved information. Each piece was a jewel.

I said, 'He raised someone from the dead, my friend. Maybe he'll give me a face, and you, too!'

"My friend asked, 'Do you have anything to eat?' I passed him my radish.

"We heard many footfalls up the road, and hosannas and cheers. My friend started calling out for alms. As the crowd grew closer, he cried louder.

"The hosannas came upon us. And as people walked by, we knew people were coming up to us, but the shouting made it hard to hear the clinks of coins dropping onto our rag. My friend raked his fingers through the coins and said, 'This is a good day!' He kept shouting for alms.

"I started to holler, too. I hollered, "Jesus! Have mercy on me Jesus!'

"My friend tried to make me quiet. People in the road scolded me. They said that it was base to bellow at a great man of God. Some said so heatedly. A couple of stones struck the ground behind me and skipped on. I think they were meant only to scare.

"But someone else said, 'Let him alone, let him shout! It is the Lord's doing!" I kept shouting for Jesus to have mercy on me.

"Then someone said, 'Cheer up! Jesus is calling you to him.'

"I grabbed my walking stick and stood up. But I couldn't go forward; my friend was holding the tail of my cloak. I threw off my cloak and walked forward.

"This was terrain I knew well. I knew the short downward slope from the tree to the road. The dirt and grass became fitted stones where the road started. The road was smooth, so it was easy to walk on it.

"The difficulty was the number of people. I walked slowly in the direction that people urged me to go, toward Jesus. With my free hand, I felt my way through the crowd. Sometimes, out of nowhere, a hand would grab me and guide me up the road.

"There was shouting, but as I got closer to Jesus the noise died down. Finally, there was silence, and I knew that

I had come into his presence. He had stepped off the road, so when I came to him, I stood on grass.

"But I didn't know exactly where Jesus stood until he said, 'What do you want me to do for you?' He was right in front of me.

"I said, 'Teacher, let me see again.'

"He said, 'Go. Your faith has healed you.'

"At first, there was nothing – neither light nor darkness. But suddenly, there was brilliant whiteness. This amazed me.

"I turned my head in different directions with my eyes wide open. Then I looked up. When I did that, I quickly became aware of the color blue. I started to grin.

"Then I looked down and saw green where my feet were.

"I look up again and saw a dove fly across my field of vision. I shouted, 'A bird!' When I shouted that, people cheered.

"I continued to explore my surroundings with my eyes. I saw faces around me, people in the crowd.

"Then I turned back to Jesus.

"He did not look like I expected.

"There were more cheers and shouts of exultation. People thumped me with the flats of their hands and grabbed my arms and hands and touched me. I marveled at being able know before someone touched me or grabbed me that they were about to do that.

"It was like a dream. I laughed, and I shouted for joy. People said, 'The Lord has done great things for you!'

"Later, I stood on the Mount of Olives and saw the walls of Jerusalem, and the Temple within its walls. I felt the same exultation.

"On the day we got to Jerusalem, Jesus and his followers went to the Temple. Outside the Temple grounds, Jesus pressed his hand against a huge, sand-colored block of stone in the eastern wall.

"A disciple came back to me and said I should walk with the disciples next to Jesus. I walked just behind Jesus, and I saw what he saw.

"After we climbed the monumental staircase leading to the southern entrance, Jesus paused inside the double gates. He examined the two domed ceilings, one after another, at the beginning of the passages under the Royal Stoa. The domes were wonderfully engraved with flowers and patterns.

"Jesus walked around the spectacular Royal Stoa, a very long building with four very long, parallel rows of pillars. Money-changers had tables there, and merchants sold animals and birds for sacrifice. Jesus dealt with them.

"Then we walked around the Court of the Gentiles. It seemed wrong to say anything, because Jesus was so absorbed with what he saw.

"Before we passed from the Court of the Gentiles to the Court of the Women, he looked for a time at the carved stones that warned gentiles to go no farther, at peril of death.

"He examined the Court of the Women, with its pillars and its four chambers in its corners. It was where money for the Temple was collected. There were beautifully-carved wooden boxes for gifts to the Temple. Each carved box was different. Jesus pointed out to us a poor widow. She was putting two tiny copper coins in the collection boxes. Jesus said that she gave more than all of the rich persons who were giving gold and silver. I don't think she heard what Jesus said.

"It was late, and the musicians were leaving.

"We went up the twelve semi-circular steps in the Court of Women, to the Nicanor Gate. We passed through that gate to the Court of the Israelites. A few people were watching from there to see the priests burn sacrifices on the high alter in the Court of the Priests. The sun was behind the Temple.

"The Temple itself is tall. The east-facing front, which was toward us, is covered with gold. The first doorway is 70 feet high, and half that in width.

"The next pair of doors inside the temple is covered with gold panels. Next to these doors are pairs of free-standing columns. These are beautifully decorated with gold grapevines and flowers. A Babylonian tapestry hangs in that doorway, hiding the sanctuary.

"Behind the sanctuary is the meeting-place of God.

"I suppose that Jesus adored the Temple for many reasons. One was that he himself had built things. Making was in his nature, like his father and his father above.

"We left the Temple and went to the Mount of Olives to sleep. I woke from time to time and gazed at the stars.

"In the next days, I saw wonderful things.

"But then, in the Garden of Gethsemane, soldiers and temple police came for Jesus.

"They crucified him at Calvary. I can't bear to think of what I saw and heard, and I won't say. Except that, at the last, he made a great shout.

"Afterward, I came up to the cross. I held his foot with my hand. It was cold, and when I pulled my hand away, blood came away with it.

"It was over.

"After that, I rued my eyes until the day that I doubted them because I could not believe what I saw. When I believed again, the joy I had was greater than the joy of getting back my sight.

"In the years since then, I have traveled far to proclaim faith in the risen Christ.

"When I went back to Jericho, I could not find my friend. Nobody knew where he had gone.

"So in addition to proclaiming Christ crucified and risen, I also seek my friend. I never saw him when we sat together by the road. But he has my cloak. He might tell the story of how he got it.

"He can keep the cloak. My Lord wants his love."

Afterword

I am the tenant farmer of these stories.

Multitudes came first. In a church study-group, we were examining the book of Luke. The group leader challenged us to imagine the life of the Gadarene (or Gerasene) Demoniac after Jesus freed him. That was the start of this book.

For *Multitudes*, I researched courtship customs in the First Century, the geography and populace of the Decapolis, the architecture of the Jerusalem Temple, and other things. Every story called for research. I'm not an expert in Church history in the First Century. I hope that I got it mostly right.

My self-editing process forced me to yank distracting elements from these stories. For example, I took out gaudy metaphors that did nothing to improve the story. Sometimes I replaced attention-seeking prose with simpler prose. If you find these defects still in these stories, believe me, it could have been worse.

Sometimes I took these stories in directions that later I regretted. I changed them accordingly.

I have had the help of friendly advice. I thank my church's book club for reading through some of these stories with me before this book was published.

These stories contain elements of my life. They contain elements of the lives of people I know, am close to, or have been close to. Of course, even when real people inspire elements of a character, the character on a page is a new creation.

These stories have ministered to me. The effort of writing them has helped me understand things that I needed to know more about. The act of writing has been a joy.

I sincerely hope that these stories have ministered to you, too.

B.Z. Eliphaz

www.ingramcontent.com/pod-product-compliance
Lightning Source LLC
Chambersburg PA
CBHW020544030426
42337CB00013B/967